WRITING
RELATIONSHIPS

WRITING RELATIONSHIPS

What *REALLY* Happens
in the Composition Class

LAD TOBIN

BOYNTON/COOK
HEINEMANN
Portsmouth, NH

Boynton/Cook Publishers, Inc.
A Subsidiary of Reed Publishing (USA) Inc.
361 Hanover Street
Portsmouth, NH 03801
Offices and agents throughout the world

An earlier version of Chapter 2 appeared in *College English* 53 (3):333–348 (Copyright © 1991 by the National Council of Teachers of English). Reprinted with permission.

An earlier version of Chapter 3 appeared in *To Compose: Teaching Writing in High School and College, Second Edition,* edited by Thomas Newkirk (Heinemann, a Division of Reed Publishing (USA) Inc., Portsmouth, NH, 1990). Reprinted with permission.

Library of Congress Cataloging-in-Publication Data

Tobin, Lad.
  Writing relationships : what really happens in the composition class / Lad Tobin.
    p.   cm.
  Includes bibliographical references (p.   )
  ISBN 0–86709–322–6
  1. English language—Rhetoric—Study and teaching. 2. English language—Composition and exercises—Study and teaching. I. Title.
PE1404.T63   1993
418'.007—dc20   92–40759
                                                                                CIP

Cover design by Jenny Jensen Greenleaf
Printed in the United States of America on acid free paper
93   94   95   96   97   10   9   8   7   6   5   4   3   2   1

Contents

Acknowledgments

People write most successfully when they enjoy supportive and stimulating relationships with teachers and peers. At least that is what I'm suggesting in this book and so it is especially fitting that I acknowledge the people whose friendship and support have helped me in my own writing.

Most of this book was written while I taught composition and directed the writing center at Saint Anselm College. During those years, I was supported by a number of good friends, including Kenn Walker, Dan Reagan, Denise Askin, Father Peter Guerin, Mary Singer, Ed Gleason, Alan Crowley, and Gary Bouchard. I also want to thank my current colleagues in the Boston College English department, particularly Judith Wilt and Paul Lewis, for giving me the chance to create a composition program that is consistent with the ideas in this book.

Of course, if there are any people who fit the "without whom this book would not have been possible" category, it is the students at Saint Anselm and Boston College who allowed me to study and write about my relationships with them and their relationships with one another.

I am also grateful to a number of people at the University of New Hampshire, including Don Graves, who helped me with the chapter on competition in the classroom, and Bob Connors, who helped me with my research on metaphorical thinking in composition. Also, thanks to Don Murray, whose articles and books drew me into the field in the first place and who has continued to read my work, meet me for one-on-one conferences, bagels, and gossip sessions, and offer encouragement and perspective. And I have to give special credit to Tom Newkirk. While writing this book, I have counted on Tom for his support, common sense, and educational instincts.

The same is true of Philippa Stratton, my editor at Heinemann. Every single change she suggested greatly improved this book; every suggestion I made, she respected and immediately understood. Like all great editors and writing teachers, Philippa operates according to the highest principle: that is, you can't always get what you want, but if you try sometimes, you just might find, you get what you need. I also owe thanks to Libby Rankin of the University of North Dakota, whose outside review helped me understand just what I'd done to

that point and just what I still had left to do; to production editors
Joanne Tranchemontagne and Cheryl Kimball, and cover designer,
Jenny Jensen Greenleaf, whose talent and patience I appreciated
throughout the production process; and to Alan Huisman, whose
sensitive and expert copyediting made my sentences much more
graceful than the ones I gave him to work with (or more graceful than
the ones with which I gave him to work?).

I want to mention, also, the contributions of my friend Randy
Albers, who helped me develop and refine many of the ideas in this
book; the Fund for the Improvement of Postsecondary Education,
particularly my project director Jay Donahue, who generously supported the research on computers and coauthoring that appears in
Chapter 8; and Eric Lister, who helped me clarify my ideas about the
relationship between psychotherapy and the teaching of writing.

Beyond all this professional help, I am lucky enough to have a
large, generous, and amazingly insightful reading group of family
members. A number of them—including my brothers, Joe and Dan
Tobin, my father, Arnold Tobin, and my father-in-law, Fred Gordon—
have gone way beyond the call of family duty by reading and
responding to drafts of chapters in this book. My mother, though,
deserves special credit: although I did not know it as a child and
would not have admitted it as an adolescent, she is the person who
first interested me in writing, teaching, and analyzing interpersonal
relationships.

Finally, I want to thank my wife, Toby Gordon, and my daughters,
Lucy and Emma. What I owe each of them so far exceeds anything I
could say in this public context that I feel embarrassed even to try.
Still, I want readers to know how much Toby helped with this book:
she has offered me encouragement, perspective, down-to-earth common sense, editorial expertise, honesty, and crucially important pep
talks. Without her support I could not have done it. Of course without
Lucy and Emma I probably could have done it much sooner, but then
it would not have meant even half as much.

Chapter One

How Classroom Relationships Shape Reading and Writing

I'm tired and ready to go home; of course, I thought I was tired and ready to go home this morning, after teaching two sections of Freshman Composition and one of Literary Theory. But that was nine conferences ago. And that was before I read some awfully rough drafts on why the drinking age should be lower, why a dog really is a man's best friend, why affirmative action is just legalized discrimination against white people, and why it is a fate worse than death to go with your parents on a family vacation. It was also before I read a comically inaccurate plot summary of William Faulkner's "A Rose for Emily" and what I'm almost certain is a Cliff's Notes interpretation of Joseph Conrad's *Heart of Darkness.*

At these moments I usually think about Don Murray's article on writing conferences ("Listening"), the one in which he talks about waiting for his last conference of a long day and realizing how lucky he is to have this job, about how he can't believe he actually gets paid to learn amazing things about other people, other worlds. When I first read that, I was a bit skeptical or maybe a bit jealous. But I've learned over the years that Murray is right: our expectations about teaching are largely self-fulfilling. The teaching of writing is enormously exciting only if we expect it to be, that is, only if we expect our students to write interesting essays, only if we read and listen carefully between the lines, only if we are honest with them and with ourselves. But it's tough to remember all this at 4:35 on a dark winter afternoon when I'm ready to go home and I still have one conference to go.

1

I get up to check the sign-up list on the outside of my door for about the tenth time today, hoping that I've had a cancellation. But I find Polly, my **4:45** appointment, already there studying the list. "I think my conference is now. Am I too early? I am a little early. Should I come back in a few minutes? I can just wait outside." I reassure her that it's fine, but she still seems tense, in a manic kind of way. "My first essay is really terrible. I don't know if you should even read it. It's terrible. I couldn't think of anything to write about. It's about the day my parents finally agreed to let me get a kitten. It was just this summer, right before I started college. That's not a good topic for an essay, is it? Sarah—she's my roommate—she read it and said it was great, but she says everything I do is great, so I don't know. Maybe you should just go ahead and read it." She gives it to me and I start to read. "I'm so embarrassed," she whispers and then theatrically covers her face with her hands. I try to reassure her: "Oh, come on, I'm sure it's not that bad."

As a matter of fact, the essay *is* that bad—all sorts of references to how cute and cuddly and adorable the kitten was. It is the sort of essay that I might have (read: would have) sneered at when I first started teaching writing. But I've learned to be more patient with developing writers and their drafts. So I stay quiet, trying to think of something to say that would indicate my displeasure with the essay without hurting her feelings. Apparently she can't stand the silence—or the tension: "I know it's really stupid. Think I should switch my topic? I know I should switch. I mean Ben writes about the homelessness problem and Cathy writes about her grandmother's funeral—it's really great, she showed it to me in the dorm—and *I* write about my kitten."

I try to get her to relax and to talk about why she had chosen that topic. She says she doesn't know but she guesses it was because she thought the kitten was so cute and because she was so surprised that her parents finally wanted to get a pet. "They never let me have one when I was little and then right before I leave for college, they finally decide to get me a kitten. It's so weird." It does seem a little weird so I push her to speculate about her parents' motives. For awhile she stumbles around, taking guesses she then immediately rejects. I begin to get discouraged but for some reason I start to sense that I—she—is onto something. Then suddenly, out of nowhere, she gets it: "I know this is going to sound absolutely crazy, but in some way, do you think that they got the kitten because I was leaving home and they wanted the cat to sort of hold my place for me in the family?"

I tell her that it does not seem crazy at all, that in fact it makes great sense. Now I am excited; I can see an evolving draft in which the kitten would become a powerful symbol. I launch into a speech about the possibilities of that essay and then, expansively, about why the process of writing is so exciting. I catch myself when I realize that Polly isn't listening; she is crying. "I mean, I never really thought about why they kept making such a big deal about the kitten until now. At the time I was even a little jealous of the kitten. Oh God, this is ridiculous. Now I really am embarrassed. I'm sorry to do this to you. I am so sorry."

But she can't compose herself. "I'm so homesick. It's so weird because I was the one of all my friends who couldn't wait to leave for college and all my friends were so nervous about it. I mean, I felt like they were all so immature. And now everyone here seems to be having a great time and *I'm* the one who is feeling homesick." She is still crying. I tell her that everyone has trouble adjusting to college, that I had a terrible case of homesickness when I first moved into a dorm. No response. I feel awkward, clumsy. She seems mortified with embarrassment. I hope that Kenn Walker, the professor in the next office, has his door shut and cannot hear her crying or my pitiful attempts at consolation. I worry that my emphasis on personal, even confessional, narrative writing has pushed Polly further than she wanted to go. I wonder if I should suggest that she might want to talk to someone in the counseling department. Or if I should move the discussion back to textual features of her essay.

"Do you think I should change my topic?" she finally asks. I wonder how she wants me to respond. She saves me by getting up to leave. "Oh, I don't know. Could I keep working on this?" I tell her that seems like a good idea.

Why Focus on Relationships? (I)

I'm telling this story not because it represents a typical moment in my writing class. Indeed, my remembering the story and my choosing to tell it suggest that in many ways it is *not* typical. Very few of my students experience epiphanies in the middle of a conference. And, fortunately, even fewer leave my office in tears. If I were describing a typical moment in one of my classes, the students might be working in small groups or I would be listening in conference to a student read a strikingly dispassionate first draft about euthanasia or rock music or, maybe, "Bartleby" or "Once More to the Lake" and I would be thinking about how to get one of us to work up some energy or emotion.

Still, the issues that my interaction with Polly raises—about writing and reading and about the interpersonal relationships that I have with my students, that they have with each other, and, finally, that I have with my colleagues—are present in less dramatic forms in every single secondary and college English class. They are issues that we rarely discuss in faculty lounges or study as research projects and ones that cannot be adequately discussed by focusing primarily on "product" (e.g., "Her essay lacks three clear subpoints to support its thesis" or "His language is ridden with clichés and truisms") or "process" (e.g., "She is having trouble with task representation" or "He needs to work harder to find his true voice").

If we want to understand what is happening in Polly's essay and in writing instruction in general, we need to pay more attention to the context in which her writing and my reading occur. Calls for focus on context are certainly not new in composition studies. Even before the relatively recent emphasis on invention as a social act (see James Berlin, Karen Burke LeFevre, and Patricia Bizzell, for example), there has been tremendous interest in our field in how context shapes composing.

Many practitioners, including Peter Elbow, Kenneth Bruffee, and Don Murray (*Writer*) have long suggested that student writing would improve if teachers played a less authoritarian role in their interactions with students and fostered more supportive student-student relationships. Others, including Robert Brooke and Muriel Harris, have focused on the ways in which teachers and students play various roles within the conference and classroom. And there have even been several studies—most notably ones by Linda Flower ("Cognition") and Les Perlman—that purport to deal explicitly with the effect of context on student writing processes.

But though composition specialists have focused on context, the language of this research tends to be either overly general and vague or overly technical, the situations too far removed from actual students and teachers. These examples are unfortunately typical:

> The essential activity in writing instruction is the textual transactions between students. These transactions should be so managed by the network as to encourage a sense of group knowledge, a sense that every transactor influences and is influenced by such group knowledge, and a sense that such group knowledge is properly malleable (responsive to the influences of each transactor). The result of textual transactions so managed is a deneutralizing of text itself and a greater emphasis and skill on the part of the transactor in rendering such text. (Barker and Kemp 15)

> For the New Rhetoric, knowledge is simply a static entity available for retrieval. Truth is dynamic and dialectical, the result of a process involving the interaction of opposing elements. It is a relation that

is created, not pre-existent and waiting to be discovered. The basic elements of the dialectic are the elements that make up the communication process—writer (speaker), audience, reality, language. Communication is always basic to the epistemology underlying the New Rhetoric because truth is always truth for someone standing in relation to others in a linguistically circumscribed situation. (Berlin 56)

Just as Kate Ronald has criticized Berlin's work on social construction because it is written in a tone and form that do not allow readers to work with him to construct *his own* text, I am criticizing the work on context because it seems eerily and airily decontextualized. In other words, most of this work is too general or too formulaic to get at the subtle, emotionally charged interactions of composition classes. What I am attempting to describe, identify, and analyze is the interactive, dialectic nature of context as it manifests itself in classroom writing relationships, as it manifests itself, for example, in Polly's conference.

The issues raised by Polly's essay are usually not covered by "context" or at least by "what we talk about when we talk about context." It may well be the case that "all meaning is socially constructed" or that Polly "fails to understand the tropes and conventions of the discourse community she is trying to enter," but those general proclamations offer little help to me or any other classroom teacher as she walks into Monday morning's English class.

Although it sometimes seems as if researchers have examined almost every tiny aspect of the composing process, there is just not much out there about interpersonal relationships and the teaching of writing. Perhaps as an overreaction to decades of microanalysis of the individual writer (Don Murray's conferences and Linda Flower's protocol analyses are prototypes here), we have leapt over relationships to macrotheories about social construction, discourse communities, women's ways of knowing, sociocognitive theory, and cultural critique. But none of this theory gets at why Polly and I both felt the way we did during those final seconds of her conference.

I think we need a way to talk about these issues—without, of course, forgetting that our primary job is to help our students become better writers. My argument in this book is that we can accomplish this by looking more carefully than we have so far at the interpersonal classroom relationships—between the student and teacher, between the student and other students, and, finally, between the teacher and other teachers—that shape the writing and reading processes.

Consider, for example, how this emphasis on classroom relationships changes the way a teacher or researcher could read Polly's essay and conference. Suppose that instead of focusing on the structural and mechanical flaws in Polly's essay, the faulty process she used to produce the text, or the conventions of academic discourse she ignored, we first examined factors that are usually considered extraneous or trivial in the teaching of writing: the tension Polly and I both felt during the conference about her weak writing and powerful emotions; my disappointment in the essay that I read; my excitement about the essay that I "misread"; our mutual fear and embarrassment that our respective peers might overhear her crying; her competitive feelings toward the students that she felt wrote on more important topics; my concern that my preoccupation with personal narrative had led to her embarrassment and pain; her sophisticated analysis of her roommate as an unreliable reader; and so on.

I am arguing that these issues are not peripheral or secondary to the writing process or the teaching of writing; they are central. Or to put it another way: traditionally we have considered the quality of the relationships in a writing classroom to be an effect of a student's success or failure as a writer; I think that it is often the other way around, that writing students succeed when teachers establish productive relationships with—and between—their students. It makes sense, then, for a writing teacher to focus as much on questions of authority and resistance as on invention heuristics and revision strategies, as much on competition and cooperation as on grammar and usage.

I can hear my critics' objections. They will tell me that I brought these problems on myself by encouraging, even requiring, my students to write personal narratives in which they search for truth and meaning and revelation. And they will point out that this is precisely why composition should focus on academic discourse and on research writing rather than self-actualization and confessional prose. And, finally, they will remind me, not everyone has the time to meet in one-to-one conferences or to worry about interpersonal relationships.

But it's not just my critics who will tell me this. My editor, Philippa Stratton, already has. She told me she liked my kitten story, but even as she said it I knew there was a "but" coming eventually. (After all, I'm a writing teacher. I know the tricks: "Always say something positive about a text before you criticize it".) She continued slowly: "This example might work . . . for those *already* in the 'process' camp" (she was being kind here: one outside reviewer described it as the "so soft it almost squishes" camp), *but* for teachers who do not rely so much on personal writing and individual conferences . . . there might be problems." And to back this up, she showed me a comment from another outside reviewer: "I had a negative reaction to the Polly example. Polly, the kitten, etc.—yes, *I* can relate to it, *did* in fact, but in the current scholarly climate, it's risky to begin with this."

"So you can see," Philippa concluded, "there's a lot for you to mull over."

But I did not want to mull things over. Like my students, I wanted to know my grade right then. I wanted to be told by my editor that my writing was wonderful. And I wanted to resolve immediately whatever tensions existed between us and within my text. She, however, wanted to keep the writing and revision process alive: "My sense," she explained, "is that you may not want to do *quite* what the outside reviewers suggest, but their responses may help you figure out just what it is you do want to do . . . . Let's talk about this again once you've had time to mull it over." Damn. I thought I had already figured out what it was I wanted to do. Before this discussion, I thought I was happy with my text. But writing for an editor—like writing for a teacher—is not just about being happy with our own texts; it's also about power and authority, identification and resistance, negotiation and compromise. (You know the old song: "I want to be happy/But I won't be happy/'Til I make you happy too.")

I could see her point, which is probably why I felt so defensive. But *my* point was that the dynamics of interpersonal relationships shape reading and writing in *all* English classes—not just in ones that employ process teaching, personal narratives, and one-to-one conferences. Whether a student is writing a new critical explication of "Because I Could Not Stop for Death," an argument about affirmative action laws, or even a lab report on a water pollution experiment, these issues are always present, always shaping how we as teachers read and respond, and how they as students write and rewrite. And how editors respond ("If you want to reach more than just the process audience, it might help to start with an example about academic writing and classroom dynamics") and how writers respond to an editor's response ("OK, but I still want to start with an example where these tensions are especially intense and dramatic").

So, with that writing relationship intact for the moment, let me start over with a different example:

By midterm I thought I finally had him pegged: Steve was going to get by in this class—no doubt about that—but he wouldn't put himself out too much. He never said a word in class unless I called on him directly. And even then he always answered in a way that indicated that he didn't think much of my question. He always sat at the last desk in the semicircle, pushed up against the wall. He had cultivated, even perfected, the minimalist style that some teenagers adopt when they are forced against their will and mental health to spend time with adults, especially adults in authority. But all of this was before I read his essay about the labor conflict at the Maine shipyards.

We had discussed his idea for that essay in a conference. "Could I do my research paper about a thing that happened last year at the shipyard where I work each summer? There was a fight between some of the shipbuilders and some of the fabricators; fabricators are the workers who prepare the metal for the shipbuilders. Anyway, each group has its own union and its own way of doing things and I could write about that." Since I always encourage students to go beyond the STANDARD RESEARCH PAPER, since I am always pleased when a student brings his own experience into his writing, and since the whole union struggle seemed like a rich topic, I encouraged him. I suggested that he might put the fight into a larger context, do some library research on labor unions in the shipbuilding industry. "And you could interview some of the workers when you are home at Thanksgiving." I expected something better than his usual essays; still, when I asked him that day if he would read his introduction aloud to the class, I had no idea what was coming.

> The smell of the fish. The little red and yellow compact cars built for people who really have no place to go would carry the smell up the hill with their wind, so when a whole caravan of Massholes would rush by on their way to a better life at Popham Beach State Park there would be a huge wave of rotting yellowish fish flesh in their wake.
>
> They'd dump it right at the side of the road, the oil from the ground fish flesh that kids had thrown up on the highway dripping off their bumpers. The smell would hang around all afternoon because there was no wind.
>
> Some of the Massholes would slow down and point us out to their children, point us out and say things like "working for a living" and "just a high school diploma." And then they'd drive away into the sunset, feeling like they'd educated their children that day.

I was hooked right away. I was a bit taken aback by the portrait of the fish-vomiting "Massholes"—a reference to wealthy Massachusetts residents who vacation on the Maine coast—but I was impressed with the sound and rhythm of the writing and with the edginess of the narrative. I could tell it was influenced by the Tom Wolfe essays we had discussed in class the previous week; I could hear the influence in the tone and in the repetition of phrases and grammatical structures. (Later I found out from Steve that he had decided to try to write a "Tom Wolfe–type essay" after he heard Brendan—the student with the peer reputation as the best writer in the class—read his own "new journalism" piece on his experience as an army reservist during the Gulf War.)

I hesitated but asked Steve to keep reading. I had planned to work on leads and intros by asking several students to read the first paragraph of their research essay and then talking about what makes an effective introduction. I had brought in several—some from students in past years, some from famous essays—that I wanted to use as examples of effective and ineffective introductions. But by hooking me, his lead had ruined that plan. Still, my lesson plan wasn't the only reason for my hesitation. I also sensed that if I came on too strong I might scare Steve away. Though I know this seems an odd metaphor, I sensed that I needed to approach him the way I might approach an animal I suddenly came upon in the woods: he might let me get close as long as I pretended that I didn't notice or care about his presence.

And there was one more issue: by asking Steve to read more, right after not asking the first two students who read from their essays to read more, right after telling the class that we would only read introductions, I was sending the message that I preferred his piece to the others. Now that is not inherently bad (I *did* prefer his lead), but I have learned the hard way—as a teacher and then as a returning graduate student—that a teacher's publicly stated preferences carry tremendous weight in a writing class. In the end my curiosity overwhelmed my caution, so I asked him to keep reading.

> The big sign that hung outside the big gate into the big yard said "Through these gates pass the best FABRICATORS in the world." Down the road there was a big sign that read "Through these gates pass the best SHIPBUILDERS in the world."
>
> The SHIPBUILDING union men used to come up and talk down to the FABRICATION union boys, joking and prodding about the fish smell and the miserably hot and stuffy little tar paper shack that stood leaning against a tree outside the big gate, joking and prodding about how cool it was back in town, back at the air-conditioned SHIPBUILDER union house, laughing and poking each other in the back about the little faded, hand-drawn sign that was nailed to the tree outside. "Local Union #6." They'd pretend to not want to leave, hesitating on the steps and saying things like "jeez, gonna be a scorcha huh?" and "shit, sure does get hot out here don't it." And then they'd get back into their air-conditioned SHIPBUILDER union pickup and drive away to a cool SHIPBUILDER union house.

I knew from our conference that Steve intended to focus on the violence that grew out of the tensions between the two unions, so I stopped him for a second to point out to the class how effectively he was setting up this opposition right from the start. He read several more paragraphs that skillfully demonstrated this point. The shipbuilders got fresh coffee; the fabricators had to drink instant. The shipbuilders got the fresh morning papers; the fabricators read already-thumbed-through news. And so on.

I asked the class if they thought this was a good introduction. The consensus was that it was better than good, though Polly said she wasn't sure if she understood a lot of it and Ray wanted to know what the "Massholes" had to do with it all, anyway. "I tie that in a little in the next paragraph," Steve explained. "I keep bringing them in to show how people outside the shipyard look at the workers."

> The fish were smelling really bad the day the new *SHIPBUILDER* union man came by to drop off the previous day's papers, an unusually large amount of Massholes with dead fish dripping off their bumpers had already driven by, leaving big piles of squished and oily fish flesh on the side of the road. He drove up in the brand new *SHIPBUILDER* union truck and parked right in front of the big gate, and when he got out he looked at the big sign that read "Through these gates pass the best FABRICATORS in the world" and he laughed.

Here I got really excited. "So are you are trying to show the irony of it all: the shipbuilders resent the Massholes for looking down on them but then they go ahead and do the same sort of thing to the fabricators? Isn't that what you're saying?"

"I never really thought of it like that," he answered glumly.

I wanted to press on and tell him that of course he thought of it like that, it was there in his paper, just waiting to be fleshed out; but I have learned that what I see that is right there waiting and what a student sees are not always—or ever—identical. Anyway, he said, the Massholes were in the paper mostly to set a mood; the paper was really about the violence that broke out between the fabricators and the shipbuilders, violence that drew the attention of the local and even national press.

By this point, I was feeling pretty proud of Steve and of myself. Obviously he deserved credit for his skill and daring and effort. But I had decided that I was the one who gave him the room and encouragement and the freedom to discover himself. I was the one who had resisted the tired research paper formats that my less inspired, less creative colleagues still clung to. And it had paid off. This was great. This was a breakthrough. This was just the sort of moment when I should have been looking over my shoulder.

Because at just this moment Steve explained that the "Massholes" only appear in his introduction and conclusion; in between, he explained, he describes the fight through the perspective of two other characters: one is "a small black kid who hangs around the shipyard keeping a diary about what he sees" and "one is this little

Jewish reporter who comes up from the big city to cover the story."
As my stomach dropped and my heartbeat took off, I asked him to
read a bit of that part and found to my horror that the momentum
of his hip, rhythmic narrative was carrying him and us toward what
seemed to me to be some fairly ugly racial and ethnic stereotypes.
And I was even more unsettled when I began to suspect, no, I *knew*
(though I don't think I can explain exactly *how* I knew), that the
streetwise, homeless, and to my mind stereotypical African American kid was supposed to be Steve—who in fact is actually a white
middle-class kid from a small town in Maine—while the fast-
talking, ambitious, rumpled little Jewish reporter with the frizzy
black hair and big nose was supposed to be me—though my hair is
curly not frizzy, and my nose is not all *that* big.

In a scene that I assume was meant to symbolize our last conference—a conference in which I apparently responded with less enthusiasm than Steve wished for—the little black kid shows his diary to
the reporter, who quickly reads it and dismisses its importance, all
the while spitting pieces of pastrami over the pages. I was suddenly
caught in one of those moments when I wish I could stop the video
for a minute or two to think. Clearly something was wrong here but
I wasn't quite sure how to respond. I was angry and I was hurt and I
was extremely surprised. I did not think my responses to Steve or his
reading had been insensitive or mean, but apparently our relationship was more complicated and more loaded than I realized. Caught
off guard, I wasn't sure if I should be objecting first to (what I took to
be) his racism, his anti-Semitism, or his personal attack on me. I
wasn't even sure if I should be objecting in front of the other students.

When one of his classmates asked him to read the end, I was glad
for the extra time to think. Unfortunately it is hard to think and listen
at the same time (though I try to do it each time I hold a writing
conference). I was angry and agitated. I raced through all sorts of
possible responses. I could ignore it for now and discuss it with
him in his conference the next week. Or I could call him on his
anti-Semitism right there in front of the class, leaping to my feet,
pointing, and yelling, *"J'accuse!"* Or I could flat-out fail him and then
mockingly suggest that if he wanted to file a complaint he could call
the antidefamation league.

By now Steve was reading his conclusion to the adoring masses,
and—again unfortunately—the writing was terrific.

> The article that the Jewish reporter wrote about the fight was read
> in the Big City and talked about by all the imaginary empathizers
> and dinner-table sympathizers and the whole Big City issued one
> very long and concerned sigh over the whole situation before simul-

taneously hopping back on their treadmills and exercise bicycles and renewing their march toward a better life.

The article wasn't read by the FABRICATION union boys as they sat out on the ground in the morning before it got too hot and drank watery coffee, and it wasn't read by the SHIPBUILDER union men as they drove laughing down the six mile stretch of road to shit on the FABRICATION union boys, eating their Dunkin' Donuts pastries and spilling their McDonald's coffee all over themselves in their laughter. The closest the article got to them was maybe if the little teeny-bopper attendant at Dunkin' Donuts was reading it and set it down to get three apple and two cherry pastries for some of the SHIPBUILDER union men or if one of the thousands of Massholes that drove by used it to wipe the dead fish flesh off their windshields and threw it on top of the oily piles on the side of the road where it stuck, but not any closer.

I asked for responses and questions from the class.

"I loved it."

"The writing is great."

"Did that really happen?"

I broke the mood. "There is some wonderful stuff in here, but I'm uncomfortable with the portrait of the black kid and of the Jewish reporter," I started out. "I know you don't mean for them to be offensive—racist or anti-Semitic, I mean . . . but . . . I'm really uncomfortable with what you're doing." I hesitated because I sensed resistance, even resentment, in the room. From Steve and from the class. I felt cornered. I had pushed creativity, risk taking, and personal voice. Steve's essay had all of that. And here I was criticizing it.

"Steve, maybe we should talk about this later in a conference? Could I talk to you for a minute during group time?" I asked nervously. I wanted to indicate publicly that I was unhappy but I did not want to put him too much on the spot in front of his peers.

After dividing the class into small peer response groups, I asked Steve if he'd like to step out in the hall with me for a minute—a request, I realize now, that sounds more like the invitation to a barroom fight than to a productive teacher-student conference. I sensed he was worried. I know that I was. I began to wonder if I was overreacting. The essay did contain some wonderful writing and information, and, after all, the whole tone of the essay was "literary" and comical. Didn't that allow him some slack in his portraits of the "characters"? Was I being thin-skinned? And what if it turned out that my response had more to do with my own biases and associations than with Steve's? After all, I didn't mind his bashing when it was directed at the middle-class "Massholes"; wasn't that simply because it basically agreed with my own leftist sympathies that somehow allow me—despite my own privileged middle-class back-ground—to identify with the workers rather than with the wealthy, self-satisfied Boston tourists? But the fact remained that I was not comfortable with Steve's identification of himself as an African-American or with his image of me or of Jews in general. Still I hesitated: how much was this a question of personal politics and taste?

I knew the risks of blowing up at him. How could I keep teaching and working with Steve for the rest of the semester if I came down too hard on him now? He finally comes a little out of his shell and I accuse him of bigotry and anti-Semitism? And how would that translate to the other students? I thought about how hard I try to make my students think that I am open-minded and—I am embarrassed to admit—"cool." I thought about how often I encourage them to take risks.

Clearly the other students admired his essay. Until the point at which the black kid and Jewish reporter were introduced, I had acted as if I admired it as well. So once Steve told his classmates that I had chewed him out, wouldn't my effort to establish trust with all of them be damaged? How this looked to the other students might present Steve with problems, too. Since his classmates admired his essay and since they all now knew that I had some problem with it, wouldn't his decision to change it be seen as capitulation? Wouldn't peer pressure—which is a huge force in secondary and college writing classes—push him toward defensiveness and entrenchment?

But just as Steve probably felt his colleagues looking over his shoulder, I felt mine watching me as well. I had felt pleased, even smug, at first about the creative form and diction of Steve's essay partially because they so clearly violated the form and diction of the conventional research paper. By encouraging this sort of creative "I-Search" paper (Macrorie), I was doing my part in what I sometimes see as the battle against the forces of convention and correctness who want to control student writing and writing instruction. I thought about one of my colleagues—he is my most frequent adversary on these issues—and I imagined him saying, "I told you so." He assigns research topics to his students. He also organizes his whole composition course around the rules of grammar; around discouraging, then discovering, and, finally, punishing plagiarism; around minilessons on proper footnote indentations and one-inch margins. I thought of the former dean, who remained so supportive of our composition program primarily because he thought we were concentrating primarily on grammar and correctness and MLA rules. I thought about all these things—or at least they flashed before my eyes as we walked toward my office, which, mercifully, is just down the hall—and I felt again that I was right in allowing for, encouraging, and even demanding that students take risks in their choice of topics and forms.

But was I doing my students a disservice by allowing, even demanding, unconventional writing? Was it OK that his essay sounded more like Tom Wolfe (whom I had exalted) than like Kate Turabian or the authors of the MLA style sheet (whose importance I had minimized)? Did I only want students to take risks that I would take?

We sat down. Neither of us made eye contact. "I love the stuff about the labor dispute, but I'm uncomfortable with the way you use the black kid and the Jewish reporter."

"I didn't mean to offend anyone," he said looking like he wanted to offend me.

"I know. But I think it *will* offend some readers."

"I don't want to change it. Everyone else seemed to like it. Are you telling me that I *have* to change it?" His question gave and took away my authority in the same second.

I thought about how all the things I needed to know right then I never learned in kindergarten—or in graduate school for that matter. I didn't remember Strunk and White's dealing with any of this and a Flower and Hayes protocol analysis seemed out of the question. I glanced at him; he was looking away. His expression was halfway between nervousness and hate. When he finally glanced at my face, I'm sure he saw the same thing.

Why Focus on Relationships? (II)

For some readers this example may seem as problematic as my first one. Steve's essay can hardly be called standard academic discourse. Still, in spite of the somewhat unusual nature of Steve's essay, the problems that it raises—about assessment, about interpretation, about writing from sources, about language as social action, about group dynamics, about teacher authority and student resistance, and so on—are, I am convinced, always present. The written product and the writing process always exist within—and are always shaped by—a particular network of interpersonal relationships.

Now it might sound from all this as if I am trying to turn a course in composition—the teaching and study of writing—into pseudo-sociology or amateur psychology. "What is all this touchy-feely stuff?" my critics are complaining. "Is this a writing class or a sensitivity group?" Those same critics are probably uncomfortable focusing first not on the conventions of written discourse or on the writing process but on "relationships," a term that conjures up notions of love affairs or, perhaps, of psychotherapy, which, in turn, lead to disturbing associations about intimacy and sexual tension, power and authority, wellness and illness. To say, "But we are writing teachers, not counselors or therapists or performers" only begs the question I am asking in this book, which is: what does it mean to be a writing teacher, anyway? I am not just suggesting that establishing, monitoring, and maintaining productive relationships in the classroom would be *another* nice thing for us to accomplish if we could just find the time; I am suggesting that it is the *primary* thing we must do if we want to be successful writing teachers.

We need, in other words, to go beyond simplistic notions of the teacher-student relationship. It's not enough to talk about decentering authority, to talk about the teacher as a facilitator and students as members of a writing community, just as it's not enough to talk about the teacher as an expert and the students as novices. Anyone who has ever taught for even a week knows that the teacher-student relationship is much more complex than these models suggest. Like the relationship between parent and adolescent child, therapist and patient, entertainer and audience (and by the way, I know these analogies are "loaded"), the relationship between teacher and student is dynamic, subtle, and highly charged.

Similarly, when we examine the student-student relationship, we need to go beyond generalized notions of collaboration, discourse communities, and the social construction of knowledge. We need to discuss the complicated, powerful, and sometimes positive role that competition plays in every classroom; we need to acknowledge not only that students learn from and identify with one another but also that they define themselves *against* their peers; and we need to understand what actually occurs when we divide students into groups, tell them that they are a community of writers, and say, "Collaborate."

Finally, we need to look more carefully at the teacher-teacher relationship, at how we relate—directly and indirectly—to other teachers. While our peers are not literally in our classrooms, they are almost always present in our thoughts, assumptions, and anxieties and, I would argue, influence almost every decision we make. What classroom teacher is not somehow aware of how her pedagogical approach supports or resists the established curriculum of her school system or principal or dean or department chair? I know, for example, that throughout my tense interaction with Steve I was aware of how this argument might seem to other teachers and found myself wishing for some perspective, some collegial support. Unfortunately, though, too busy or uncomfortable to admit our deficiencies to our colleagues, we often end up facing these problems alone. To make matters worse, there is almost no published material on how a writing teacher's relationships (or lack of relationships) with other writing teachers shape his interactions with students.

Still, I want to be clear about something: this is not an either/or choice. My point is not that we should focus on these various interpersonal relationships *instead of* focusing on the product or the individual writer's process. And my point is not that we should ignore the rules of grammar, the conventions of language, or the modes of discourse; I'm simply saying that when we focus on student writing, that when we do teach rules and conventions, we need to pay attention to the specific context in which the student is writing and we are reading.

Since product, process, and context are inseparably linked, it is all a matter of where teachers or researchers decide to place the camera and of when we decide to begin filming. My goal in writing about how classroom relationships shape reading and writing—and how reading and writing shape classroom relationships—is to offer a new model for researchers by beginning to fill in the huge gap between studies of student texts that ignore context altogether and studies that define context in theoretical terms that are too general to offer any practical help to a researcher. But more importantly I am choosing to focus on relationships because I want to raise a new set of issues and questions that will help teachers when they create writing assignments; when they read, evaluate, and respond to student essays; and when they decide how to use class time.

The real question is, how can writing teachers shape these relationships to make the writing and reading processes productive for students and for themselves? My definition of a productive classroom relationship is, I think, simple enough: any relationship that fosters the writing and reading processes is productive; any relationship that inhibits them is not. My own sense is that a student and teacher can relate productively only if a certain amount of tension exists between them, only if—to borrow a model from psychologist Mihali Csikszentmihalyi—they are both somewhere between boredom and anxiety. But I don't mean to imply that there is a single model of a productive writing relationship. Since interpersonal relationships are interactive, dynamic, and dialectical, teachers need to negotiate different productive relationships with different classes and different students. What I am arguing against are prescriptive rules and roles for writing teachers, no matter what camp or position they defend.

More than rules, we need stories. And that is what I have tried to do here: to tell stories about actual situations from my classes that evoked powerful responses from me and my students. And though I am claiming that these stories are "what really happens in the composition class," I also need to acknowledge the extent to which my experiences and perceptions are shaped and limited by my own circumstances, including my gender, race, and class. Though I am trying to start an academic conversation with writing teachers in all sorts of settings—universities, community colleges, secondary schools—I am painfully aware how much my stories reflect my own experience as a white middle-class male teaching mostly middle-class Catholic students. Still, I hope that by telling stories that go beyond the happy talk of collaboration, decentered authority, and writing communities to moments like the ones with Polly and Steve—moments when I felt frustrated, angry, unsettled, lost, or bored—I will invite readers to identify their own problems and frustrations.

But this book is not an endless litany of failures. Like all relationships, writing relationships are dynamic, fluid, and multi- faceted; and like all good relationships, they can allow us\to accomplish and become all sorts of things that we could not do or be on our own. There are many moments in this book and in each semester when I realize that my students are writing unimaginatively and that I am teaching ineffectively because I have failed to establish productive relationships with and between them as writers. But there are many other moments when I realize that all students can write wonderful and surprising essays once we have discovered powerful and positive ways to relate to one another. Those realizations—and those relationships—are at the center of all the stories I tell here.

Part One

The Teacher-Student Relationship

What is a good teacher-student writing relationship? According to the language of the day, it is a relationship that empowers our students. But as Susan Hubbuch argues in a recent article, empowering does not happen by simple ordinance. And as my interaction with Steve shows, empowering is one thing; what a student does with that new power is a very different thing. The key is to think more carefully about the role we play in this relationship.

Ironically, as much as the teacher's role seems to have changed in the great paradigm shift from "product" to "process," one thing remains the same: we still have written ourselves relatively minor and unfulfilling parts to play in the writing process. In the traditional class the writing teacher played several roles—provider of information, lecturer, upholder of standards, corrector—but each was relatively static, unilateral: the teacher provided his students with rules and models of good writing and then graded them according to how closely the results approximated those rules and models. Not only did this role fail to reflect the intelligence, creativity, and interests of the student, it failed to acknowledge the intelligence, creativity, and interests of the teacher. In fact our role in the traditional classroom seems to me a little like the tyrant's role in Orwell's "Shooting an Elephant." By denying our students power, we actually limited our own freedom. Although we did most of the talking, although we told the students the rules and gave them the models, although we believed that we were in control, there was actually very little room for the sort of originality, risk taking, and inquiry that Cynthia Onore and others have argued is essential if a writing relationship is to be successful (240).

When I say that our role as writing teachers is still dull and one-dimensional, I am not suggesting that there has been no significant change over the last two decades. Nor am I ignoring current examples of more innovative and interactive teacher-student relationships. It's just that the new role that most process teachers have adopted is in many respects as narrow and rigid as the old one. I'm referring to teachers who describe themselves as "facilitators" (as if they have no agenda of their own, or rather, as if their agenda is not important) or as "just another member of the writing workshop." The concept of the decentralized writing classroom is based on the following logic (or illogic): "All we really have to do is get out of our students' way and let them write." I realize I am creating something of a caricature here of the process teacher and classroom, but I think there has been an element of naiveté in this approach.

Many writing teachers deny their tremendous authority in the classroom because it does not fit the image they would like to project. Most of us are uncomfortable admitting that we *are* the center of a "decentered" classroom, that we hold so much power, that we are largely responsible for success and, even worse, for failure. But while there are good reasons for our discomfort—many of us would like for political reasons to think of our classroom as democratic, supportive, and nonhierarchal—there are even better reasons to face the truth: from a student's perspective a writing teacher is an authority figure, even—or especially—in process classrooms. In fact, the teacher in composition classes in which students are asked to write about their personal feelings and to meet in one-to-one conferences actually holds more authority, because the stakes are higher.

I suspect that the notion of teacher as nonauthority developed as a necessary stage in or antithesis to the thesis offered by traditional classroom teachers. The synthesis or solution, though, is to move beyond either/or thinking—either we have authority or they do; either we own the text or they do; either the meaning is in the writer or in the reader—toward a more dialectical definition. Rather than dichotomizing the teacher's and the student's roles, we need to see how they are inseparably related. Just as Janet Emig argues (in "Uses") that traditional models of the composing process fail because they ignore the role and uses of the writer's unconscious, most of our current views fail because they ignore the role and uses of the teacher's (or reader's) unconscious. Until we have a clearer and more realistic notion of how we shape and influence student writing and how, in return, that writing shapes and influences us, we will continue to limit our student's potential development.

And to limit our own. One reason many composition teachers dislike teaching composition is that they feel they are supposed to dislike it and then set out to prove it. The teaching of writing should not be fun, they feel, and a writing course certainly should not be tailored to a teacher's individual taste and preference. This sense of composition as a teacher's duty or burden runs deep in our profession and is one of the reasons so many people distrust, resent, and envy those writing teachers who talk about their work in intensely personal and positive terms. I know for a fact that my colleagues are more than a little skeptical when Toby Fulwiler gloats that Freshman Writing is the "Best Course in the University to Teach" or Don Murray muses, "There must be something wrong with a fifty-four-year-old man who is looking forward to his thirty-fifth conference of the day" ("Listening" 232). This kind of enthusiasm for composition does not seem possible to teachers who have scrupulously sought to remove themselves and their own interests from the course.

In my interaction with Steve these issues came together: I wanted to help students produce livelier and riskier essays; I wanted students to resist my authority; I wanted them to find their own voices; I wanted them to bring their interests and obsessions into the classroom and into their writing. And I wanted all of this for their sake and for mine. I know from years of experience that I don't want to read another research paper on the causes of the Civil War or symbolism in *The Scarlet Letter*. I don't want students just writing to please me, writing for a grade. But giving up the teacher-as-facilitator role is almost as hard as giving up the teacher-as-authority role because it forces us to be honest about our biases and limitations and it forces us to make a lot up as we go along. In this case I needed to indicate to Steve that I personally found his comments on blacks and Jews objectionable and I needed to say this in a way that allowed him to keep what he liked, that prompted him to revise what I felt needed to be changed, and that somehow kept our relationship intact at the same time. And on top of all that, I had to think about how to grade the essay (more on that topic in Chapter 4).

Throughout the chapters in this section, I will focus on these sorts of issues, on the ways that teacher and student shape texts and each other, by focusing on different scenes in which the teacher-student relationship is negotiated and acted out: reading student essays (Chapter 2); responding to essays in a one-to-one conference (Chapter 3); grading (Chapter 4); and discussing writing with the whole class (Chapter 5).

Chapter Two

Reading Students, Misreading Ourselves, and Vice Versa

At the end of each semester I ask my students to write an essay on writing, to identify and comment on some significant feature of their own writing process. The idea is to help them better understand how they have written in the past so that they will have more control over how they write in the future. Most of my students find this assignment tedious and end up writing a fairly perfunctory self-study, but I keep giving this assignment for two reasons: first, I am really curious about how students view the writing process, and second, when these "process papers" are good, they are remarkably good.

Recently I was telling two of my colleagues about a particularly insightful essay one of my students had written about the relationship between thought and language. In her essay, Nicki argues that a writer can only think clearly when she is allowed to use a voice and a style that she has mastered. She felt that in my course, she had been able to think through important issues in original ways; however, in her humanities class, she had trouble developing and organizing her ideas about Homer, Cicero, and the Hebrew prophets. She accounts for the difference not by the difficulty of the material—she took on complicated problems in my course—but rather by the encouragement I gave her to explore ideas that mattered to her in personal and informal language. Her humanities professor, she complains, had denied her this access by insisting on numerous references to the text and "impeccable English prose."

Her point is not simply that her expression became more awkward in her humanities papers; instead, she is arguing that in the translation from her own form of expression to the academic language required in that course, her actual ideas were lost or distorted. The irony, she concludes, is that although her humanities teacher claims to value creativity and logic, he insists that students write in a form that virtually guarantees detachment and confusion. "But what is best about her essay," I told my colleagues, "is that it is so well written. At the end she writes something like, 'The essay I am writing right now proves my point. I am comfortable and I am able to use "I" and "you," which allows me to tell you clearly and directly what I think. But when I try to write 'impeccable English prose,' I lose sight of my audience and I disappear as a writer.' "

They seemed impressed, maybe even won over, by the idea of this assignment. But as I walked back to my office, I started worrying that I had overstated the value of the assignment and the quality of Nicki's essay. When I reread it, I was embarrassed to discover how much I had organized and focused her argument in my retelling. It is not as if her essay was without thought or skill. In fact, the section that I singled out for its rhetorical sophistication was actually much better in Nicki's paper than in my memory and retelling:

> In Humanities, I have to remember a certain format and I have to back up every general statement with specific examples. Oh, and that word "I," I just used. You would never see that word in one of my Humanities papers. Neither would you see "you." It would be marked with red ink and a comment, "You who???" or "To whom do you think you are referring?"

But in general the writing seemed much flatter and more prosaic than I had remembered it:

> Though it is good to be able to write for different audiences, I do not want to have to change my preference in writing because of some particular "format" I am supposed to follow. There is no law that states that I must write in a certain way. When I write I like to feel as if I have gotten across what I want to say.

But it wasn't just the writing. My discomfort grew as I began to see how much her whole argument echoed my own ideas—I, also, believe that a student should be allowed to write in her own voice, that she should be able to choose topics, that writing is a mode of thinking, and so on—all ideas to which I have a strong ideological and personal commitment. For years I have argued with colleagues who believe that students should not be allowed to write in first person or from personal experience, who insist on impeccable prose, correctness, and perfect one-inch margins. So it only makes sense that I would be pleased and excited to see that my student's writing supported and even validated my own positions and, therefore, that I would make her argument more eloquent and sophisticated than it actually was.

But there were other reasons for my misreading. This was not the first essay of Nicki's I had read. I had monitored her work all semester, and I read this final essay in terms of all our other interactions. From our conferences, I knew that her parents were first-generation Greek Americans and that she was a first-generation college student from a small, working-class town in Massachusetts. From her previous essays, I knew that during her last two years of high school she had been involved with a man in his twenties who cheated on her with other women, who was addicted to cocaine, and who once beat her up at a party. I also knew that throughout that whole relationship her worst fear was that he would break up with her. I knew that she considered herself a "good Catholic" but was shocked and angry at the Church for "never telling her the truth about God."

So when I read Nicki's essay on writing and personal voice, I was also reading Nicki herself and imagining—rightly or wrongly—that this first term of college was a crucial time in her development. I was thinking about how she ended her essay on that self-destructive high school relationship:

> To this day, I am not sure why I loved someone like that. Why was I drawn to a person who treated me so badly? I guess you could say he was my drug. He was my high and my addiction. It was hard to 'just say no,' but I finally did. I've been clean for almost six months now and I plan to stay that way.

And I was thinking about how upset she was when her humanities teacher dismissed Nicki's argument—that because God in Exodus and the Book of Job was sometimes "vengeful, jealous, and merciless," he was "more realistic" than the all-loving, perfect God the nuns had described—as superficial and reductive.

But to make matters still more complicated, I was also reading myself. I had a vested interest in thinking that my teaching and my course had provided Nicki with something she did not get in her humanities class. I had an interest in thinking that my teaching helped her feel confident about her abilities and her potential. By reading Nicki's text in such a way that it reached a self-confident and successful resolution, by making it into a text with a happy ending, I could congratulate myself not only for helping another writer succeed but also for helping another student establish her identity. And perhaps most complicated of all, by reading her in a particularly imaginative and integrated way, I could use her (as I am trying to do right now) for my own benefit in my writing and research.

Obviously the specific circumstances of my reading or, more accurately, misreading are unique—and that is part of my point. But I am also suggesting that, in many ways, my misreading illustrates common issues and problems. As teachers, we play a crucial—but generally misunderstood—role in our students' writing processes. While we have begun to understand how students compose and to develop a more comprehensive and flexible view of the unconscious forces that shape their composing, we continue to oversimplify the teacher's reading or interpretative processes. Or to put it another way, while we have come to see writing as socially constructed, we have failed to understand the teacher's role in the construction of that meaning. We need to develop a theory of reading student texts that takes into account our reading of the students themselves, of our own unconscious motivations and associations, and, finally, of the interactive and dialectical nature of the teacher-student relationship.

Reading and Misreading Student Essays

The most significant relationship in any writing course is the one between the writer and her text. But if reading and writing are reciprocal or transactional processes (Rosenblatt), we also need to develop the teacher's relation to a text. The fact that I misread Nicki's essay in certain ways is not significant in itself. After all, most of us in English studies have grown relatively comfortable with the notion that our readings are not simple or literal decodings of texts, that when we read we create and recreate, deconstruct and reconstruct. While this seems to cause shock and anguish in old-fashioned New Critics and neo-Aristotelians, most writing teachers are relatively comfortable with the idea that meaning is found not solely in the text or solely in the reader but rather in the interaction between the two. In fact, that process is at the very center of our work as writing teachers: we must misread every student text in order to help students say what we think they really mean. It is this sort of generous and deliberate misreading—readings in which we go beyond the words' literal meanings to try to draw out possibilities in a text, to imagine what the text might be trying to become—that is the basis of Shaughnessy's analysis of error, Elbow's "believing game" (*Writing Without Teachers*) and Bartholomae and Petrosky's plan to integrate reading and writing.

So far, so good. But the next step causes resistance: few writing teachers want to go so far as to admit that we actually create the meaning of our students' texts, particularly if this creative act is largely the result of our unconscious biases and associations. The problem with admitting our role as coauthor is that it violates most of our fundamental beliefs about the objectivity of the teacher, the integrity of the text, and the rights of the individual author. Yet that next step seems unavoidable, a fact not lost on those interested in the application of critical theory to the composition classroom: if great literary works are unstable and subject to multiple readings and interpretations, then how unstable is the evolving draft of an inexperienced composition student (J. Harris 158)? If every reading of Chaucer and Shakespeare is a rewriting, then how can teachers avoid becoming authors of their students' drafts (Eagleton 12)? Or, to put it another way, if a teacher is reading a text that was written specifically for him, with revisions that are a direct result of his suggestions, how can he possibly have any clear sense of where the text stops and his reading begins?

But in spite of these nagging realities, my sense is that in practice most of us still cling to the notion that our readings of student essays are somehow "objective"; that is, in spite of our knowledge of reader-response theory and deconstruction, we continue to believe that when we read student essays we are responding to some objective reality in—or noticeably missing from—the text rather than to a text we have unconsciously revised or even created. It's not as if we were unaware that we bring to our teaching of writing and our reading of student essays strong beliefs and biases. We know, for example, how we feel about abortion and gun control, how our response is more favorable to some rhetorical strategies than to others, even how we like some students much better than others. But we conveniently forget those issues and pretend we can willingly suspend those beliefs and disbeliefs. We see ourselves as neutral, objective, open-minded. We give each student an equal chance. We are ready to like essays on any topic in any mode. We just want students to find their own voices, to find themselves.

This paradigm of teacher-as-objective-reader fails to do justice to the complexity of the reading and writing processes and to our relationship to our students. When we read an essay on abortion or a presidential election, most of us go out of our way to be fair, to try to evaluate the writing for its own sake, if such a thing is even possible. But what happens when we read an essay on a seemingly "unpolitical" issue or topic about which we have powerful (and often unconscious) associations? Consider, for example, this exchange during a discussion I had recently with two other writing teachers. First teacher: "If I get one more essay on 'how I won the big high school football game,' I'll scream. I mean these guys describe each play in great detail and then show how they saved the day at the end. Yuck.

They are so self-serving and so trivial." Second teacher: "You're missing the point. Those aren't trivial at all. For an adolescent male, those games can be his most significant experiences." In part this is a gender issue: the writers of most of these sports essays and the second teacher are male, while the first teacher is female. In part it is personal: the male teacher went on to explain that he remembers high school sports as perhaps the one "pure thing" in his life, while I admitted that because my memories of high school sports include failed expectations—mine and my father's—it is for me one of the most impure things in my life.

Of course, it's not true that every reading is equally idiosyncratic and personal or that a student text does not exist until we de- and then reconstruct it. I am not suggesting that all student papers are Rorschach tests or random ink blots on the page. Clearly there is a text in the class and it is even a text for which we can—and have—developed shared criteria for evaluation. Sometimes this "interpretative community" is consciously and deliberately created (we train teachers in holistic scoring, for example); more often, though, it is the result of shared unconscious preferences or, as Lester Faigley's study of teacher preferences demonstrates, shared "unstated cultural definitions" (410). There is even a certain type of essay (I call it the autobiographical narrative of a self-actualizing event) that most of us in this interpretive community prefer. But our agreeing that a text exists and agreeing about some of the criteria for evaluation should not make us underestimate our own creative and often idiosyncratic role in the process.

My point (and it has much in common with arguments made recently by Louise Wetherbee Phelps, Robert Schwegler, and Bruce Lawson and Susan Sterr Ryan) is that we need to develop a theory of reading student drafts that reflects these issues, that allows us to acknowledge—to our students and to ourselves—that we play a central role in the composing process not only when we give our students guidelines and heuristics, not only when we suggest changes in conferences, but also when we read the essays. We need a theory of reading that takes into account the "intertextual" nature of our work; that is, a theory that acknowledges that we cannot read any student essay without unconsciously and simultaneously reading a number of other texts as well. Finally, we need a theory that allows us to recognize our limitations, to say first to ourselves, and then directly to a student, "I am not going to be a good reader of an essay on this topic. You should know that going in."

In part, then, this is a process for which we need to use and extend what we have learned about reading and analysis from critical theory. But it is more—and less—than that. The evolving student draft is not identical to the published literary work and thus requires, as Phelps and others have argued, new theories of reading and response. Our readings of student essays are contextualized in ways that readings of literary texts are not. We know the authors of these texts, we work with them, we suggest changes to them, we have something to gain if they succeed or—if we dislike the students involved—something to gain if they fail. None of this is static or linear or unilateral, but changes with each teacher and each student. Therefore, in order to develop a more dialectical theory of reading and interpretation we need to consider how readers and writers—teachers and students—interact. We will not come to understand this interaction by decontextualizing context (as I believe experimentalists often do in their research on this subject) but rather by examining our readings within the student-teacher relationship.

The Lure, Lore, and Leery(ness) of Therapeutic Models

So how do we develop this new theory of reading and interpretation? How do we write more interesting and satisfying roles for ourselves to play in the writing class? And how do we develop a clearer and more realistic notion of the ways our responses and nonresponses shape student writing? My own suggestion—and it is one that may not be particularly popular or politically correct—is that we pay more careful attention to the research and experience of psychotherapists. I am not equating composition and therapy nor am I suggesting that psychotherapeutic relationships are free from the power politics and self-deceptions that I am criticizing in the writing class. I am simply saying that it makes no sense to ignore lessons from the field in which the workings of the unconscious and the subtle dynamics of dyad relationships have been carefully and systematically analyzed. I think most writing teachers know that therapeutic models can help explain and explore the teacher-student relationship, but because they find this comparison threatening they publicly deny it. That may also explain why so many composition theorists offer instructive models from and comparisons to psychotherapy that they then immediately disown. Take, for example, this paragraph by James Moffett:

> The processes of psychotherapy and writing both require maximum synthesizing of firsthand and secondhand knowledge into a full, harmonious expression of individual experience. This calls for the removal of spells to which the person has not agreed and of which

he is unconscious. Freud asked the patient to start talking about anything that come into his head—in other words, to attempt to verbalize his stream of consciousness or externalize his inner speech. This technique presupposes that from the apparent chaos of all this disjointed rambling will emerge for analyst and patient an order, eventually "betrayed" by motifs, by sequencing, by gradual filling in of personal cosmology. Thus, if successful, the subject's cosmologizing processes, the idiosyncratic ways of structuring and symbolizing experience, stand more clearly revealed and presumably more amenable to deliberate change, if desired. The most important thing a writer needs to know is how she does think and verbalize and how he or she might . . . . Not for a moment do I suggest that the teacher play psychiatrist. The therapeutic benefits from writing are natural fallout and nothing for a school to strive for. (100–101)

What I think Moffett is saying here is, writing and psychotherapy are similar processes, but composition teachers and therapists have nothing in common. In other words, although he is unquestionably drawn to—and willing to draw from—the experience of psychotherapists, he is determined to distance himself from this model as quickly as possible. In fact, Moffett's statement is only the clearest example of the schizophrenic response that most writing teachers have to the composition-as-therapy metaphor. For example, Thomas Carnicelli, concerned about the kinds of questions and clues that promote self-discovery, first suggests that Rogerian questioning might help, but then quickly offers an artificial distinction: "The teacher's function is to lead students to adopt the teacher's values, the common criteria of good writing shared by the teacher, and the English profession, and, with certain wide variations, educated people in general. The therapist's function is to lead clients to clarify or develop their own individual values" (116). Similarly, Stephen Zelnick, in writing about conferences, admits, "I am afraid that whether we wish it or not, we become role models for our students" and "there is the romantic/sexual vibration. If it is in any way possible, conferences set going a buzz and flutter of fantasies" (49). But he then dismisses the therapeutic model altogether: "Translating student conferences into other, simpler paradigms of efficient, smooth client relations, or psychotherapeutic self-exploration impoverishes education. We can do better than that" (58).

Oddly enough, Don Murray, the writing teacher whose work seems most heavily influenced by psychotherapeutic goals and methods, is perhaps the most outspoken critic of this analogy. While Murray talks again and again about reading "my other self," about "writing to learn," about writing conferences in which the teacher listens and the student speaks, about a process that sounds suspiciously similar to making the unconscious conscious, he finds the comparison ludicrous.

> Responsive teaching is often confused with a stereotypical thera-peutic role in which the teacher always nods, always encourages, always supports, and never intervenes. That is ridiculous. . . . The conference isn't a psychiatric session. Think of the writer as an apprentice at the workbench with the master workman. (*Writer* 154)

I can't help but wonder why these writing teachers are going so far out of their way to deny a connection that they actually brought up themselves. No one claims that conference teaching equals therapy; but that there are significant differences between teaching writing and doing psychotherapy is hardly the point. Carnicelli, Zelnick, Murray, and others seem to admit that there is role modeling, sexual tension, even transference, in the teaching of writing and the teacher-student relationship, but because these things make them uncomfortable (which they should) they deny their significance and suggest that we focus on the writing process and product as if they existed in a decontextualized situation and relationship.

Still, these early attempts to link composition and therapy were valuable because they called attention to important aspects of the teacher-student relationship and paved the way for more recent essays that unapologetically take advantage of therapeutic models. I want to mention two that focus on the unconscious drives and associations that shape the way our students respond to us as teach-ers. Robert Brooke, relying heavily on Lacan, suggests that students in "response" classrooms of the type Murray and Elbow describe improve their writing because they identify with—and want desper-ately to please—the teacher, the "Subject Who Is Supposed to Know" (Brooke "Lacan" 680). The student then projects or transfers emo-tions and associations from his own early-life relationships, particu-larly with his parents, onto the teacher. Ann Murphy, relying more heavily on Freud, extends Brooke's argument by demonstrating how transference can also account for our students' occasional resistance to us, to writing, to self-knowledge, to education. Murphy argues:

> Despite their many obvious and important differences, both psycho-analysis and teaching writing involve an intensely personal rela-tionship in which two people painstakingly establish trust beyond the apparent limitations of their institutional roles, in order that both might learn and one might achieve a less marginal, more fully articulated life. (181)

While I think these essays go a long way in explaining class-room dynamics, I want to go still further and suggest that countertransference—our unconscious responses to our students or, more significantly, our unconscious responses to their unconscious responses to us—also shapes the reading and writing processes. Freud's explanation of countertransference has important implications for writing teachers:

> We have become aware of the 'counter-transference,' which arises in [the analyst] as a result of a patient's influence on his unconscious feelings, and we are almost inclined to insist that he shall recognize this counter-transference in himself and overcome it. Now that a considerable number of people are practising psychoanalysis and exchanging their observations with one another, we have noticed that no psycho-analyst goes further than his own complexes and internal resistances permit; and we consequently require that he shall begin his activity with self-analysis and continually carry it deeper while he is making observations on his patients. Anyone who fails to produce results in a self-analysis of this kind may at once give up any idea of being able to treat patients by analysis. (145)

As writing teachers, we also can go no further than our own complexes and internal resistances permit, and thus we too need to begin with self-analysis. We too need to identify the extent to which our responses to our students and their writing are not neutral or objective, the extent to which countertransference responses interfere with our ability to help students improve their writing.

If writing teachers react negatively to the suggestion that they play therapist, I assume that my recommendations—that we analyze ourselves, that we consider our own neuroses in the reading and teaching processes, that we also play patient—seem even more irrelevant and threatening. Again it's not that writing teachers are unaware that our own unconscious issues often obscure and shape our actions; it's just that we hope if we don't talk about it, it will go away. For instance, Louise Rosenblatt acknowledges that when students read and write personally, they often reveal some of their "conflicts and obsessions" (207), thereby tempting teachers to deal directly with these psychological issues. Although she points out some instances in which students have benefited from this sort of interaction, she ends up warning teachers against "officious meddling with the emotional life of their students" (207) because teachers cannot be trusted in this sort of relationship:

> Unfortunately, like members of any other group, many teachers are themselves laboring under emotional tensions and frustrations. Given the right to meddle in this way, they would be tempted to find solutions for their own problems by vicariously sharing the

student's life. They might also project upon the student their own particular preoccupations and lead him to think that he was actually suffering difficulties and frustrations that were the teacher's. Assuredly even worse than the old indifference to what is happening psychologically to the student is the tampering with personality carried on by well-intentioned but ill-informed adults. The wise teacher does not attempt to be a psychiatrist. (208)

Rosenblatt is right to point out that teachers have the power to impose themselves on their students in dangerous ways, but it is not always so easy to distinguish a teacher who is guilty of projecting his "own particular preoccupations" onto his students and "tampering with personality" from one who is emotionally engaged in his teaching and honestly interested in influencing his students' values and ideas. By attempting to edit feelings, unconscious associations, and personal problems out of a writing course, we are fooling ourselves and shortchanging our students. The teaching of writing is about solving problems, personal and public, and I don't think we can have it both ways: we cannot create intensity and deny tension, celebrate the personal and deny the significance of the personalities involved. In my writing courses, I want to meddle with my students' emotional life and I want their writing to meddle with mine. Transference and countertransference emotions are threatening because they are so powerful, but they are most destructive and inhibiting in the writing class when we fail to acknowledge and deal with them.

Reading Myself Reading My Students: A Classroom Example

Let me try to illustrate this process of identifying and using countertransference emotions with an example from my own teaching. Last fall I taught two sections of Freshman Composition; from the very first week, one section went extremely well, while the other was a nightmare. I had trouble getting the students involved in the discussions or in their own writing, and I grew increasingly irritated during class. I was especially bothered by the four eighteen-year-old male students who sat next to each other, leaning back in their desks against the wall. They usually wore sunglasses and sneakers with untied laces; they always wore baseball caps. Whenever I tried to create drama or intensity, they joked or smirked. Whenever I tried to joke, they acted aggressively bored, rolling their eyes or talking to each other. At first, I tried to ignore them, not to let them get to me. But I found that it was a little like trying not to think about an elephant. I was always aware of them, even when they were not acting out.

After two weeks, I decided that everyone was being distracted by these students, that they were responsible for the unproductive mood of the classroom. But for some reason I was not able to confront them directly about their aggressive behavior in class or their passive effort outside class. It was as if in confronting them I would be acknowledging that they were bothering me and I refused to do that, partly because I have always prided myself on my relationships with students and the comfortable, relaxed atmosphere in my classrooms. So instead of confronting them directly, I stewed inside and—I am embarrassed to admit—fantasized about revenge: "Be patient," I told myself. "Grading time will come along eventually and then you can get even. You can fail them all."

I suppose the other reason I did not confront them was that when they came for their first individual conferences, they were polite, even a bit deferential. They were emotionally detached, but they answered my questions, accepted most of my suggestions, and, except for one, even seemed somewhat grateful. Still their writing was relatively weak and I made little effort to help them improve. I read their texts looking more for problems than for possibilities. I had essentially written them off: I had decided that these four were just insecure, adolescent boys trying to act tough in class, in front of the other students; that they were not secure enough with their roles, with their masculinity, to be independent, serious, or mature; that if they wanted to get nothing out of this class, then that was fine by me; and, finally, that I would just concentrate on the other students in the class and ignore them.

But that noble plan failed miserably. It seemed that every time I would accommodate their acting out, they would raise the stakes. For example, during small-group peer response times, they would choose to work together and then spend the time talking about football or dorm parties. Even worse, if I assigned groups, they would talk about writing for a few minutes and then call over to each other across groups. I retaliated (note the aggressive language) by indirectly threatening them. I interrupted the class one day to give an angry and sarcastic speech on how anyone who was not taking the class seriously would fail and end up taking it again. I told them how sorry I would feel if that happened but that I had no choice. Although I knew that these four students would not fail—their essays were not that bad—I looked right at them when I made the threat.

Finally, one day, I snapped. I walked into class, saw them together, laughing and leaning against the wall, and in a voice that conveyed much too much anger and disgust I said, "I have never had to do this is ten years of college teaching; in fact, I left high school specifically so I wouldn't have to deal with shit like this, but you guys are completely out of control. I don't want you to sit together any more." There was an awkward silence and then one of the boys said in a mocking voice, "Completely out of control? Fine, I'll move." Another asked, "That's why you left high school?" It was an embarrassing moment because it was clear—to them and to me—that I was the one who felt out of control.

What was going on? I was usually relaxed and comfortable with students. I was reasonable. I was well liked. So the problem had to be with them. They were threatened by me, I told myself, so insecure that they had to stick together and act tough. They saw me as an authority figure and were rebelling, not only against me but against authority figures from their past. And those explanations were partially true. But that did not explain why my response was so angry. I had allowed myself to get caught up in a macho competition with these students and I was losing. Clearly this had as much or more to do with my insecurities and unconscious responses as it did with theirs.

That's when I realized the significance of my slip about high school. I had meant to say, "That's why I left high school teaching," but I had referred accidently to my own experience as a high school student. I remembered periods when I acted like these students and later periods when they were the type I felt I was competing with. And I realized how much, for whatever reasons, I was still bothered by the group behavior of adolescent males. The realization helped: by recognizing and somehow naming the source of my anger, it dissipated and became more manageable. I'm not saying I suddenly felt comfortable with these students or with their texts, but the situation now seemed within my own realm, somehow within my control.

Although this example may have more to do with my own neuroses than with composition theory, the point is that this knowledge changed the way I read these students and their texts; it helped me in my teaching and, indirectly, helped these students in their writing. I began to confront them more directly, asking them if they agreed with certain points, inviting them to criticize my readings, giving them room and an invitation, in conferences and in class, to challenge me in (what I took to be) constructively indirect ways: I encouraged them to freewrite about the course and about me. I asked them to write metaphorically about writing. I told them to push back when they felt I was pushing them too hard in a conference.

Although one of the students continued to write essays that showed little effort or commitment, the other three made significant progress. One wrote an essay in which he used the metaphor of writing as playing the drums to argue against my emphasis on revision: a writer has to revise just as a drummer has to tune his kit, but "sometimes you just have to let me play." Another wrote a satiric essay on "productive procrastination," suggesting not only that I took writing too seriously but also that my view of the process was limited and limiting. He ended his essay by saying,

> If you begin writing too early, the pressure may not be great enough. If you begin too late, your ideas will not have time to take shape. Procrastination is the key because it triggers your unconscious ideas. Oh, by the way, it is now **3:27** a.m. And you probably thought I wouldn't have time to write a good essay.

The fact that these challenges to my authority came in conventional forms that supported my authority neutralized my anger and defensiveness; the fact that I allowed and encouraged these challenges neutralized theirs.

But the third student, Jack, provided the best example of this sort of interaction. From the beginning of the year, he had seemed the angriest and the least cooperative. I was irritated that the first essay he brought to a conference, "The Advantages and Disadvantages of Biotechnology," was clearly written as a report for a high school class. When I asked him to write something new, he brought in "How to Make a Peanut Butter and Jelly Sandwich." There were attempts at humor ("A true P, B, and J expert takes this science a step further by experimenting with exotic varieties of peanut butters and jellies"), but for the most part it was a flat description of the process.

As I was reading it, he spoke up, "Remember in class what you said? You said that there are no good or bad topics, that someone could write a trivial essay on something profound, like nuclear war, or a profound one on something trivial, like making a peanut butter and jelly sandwich. So I tried it." Again I felt irritated, and couldn't quite figure out how to respond, so I asked him the purpose of the essay. "To tell the reader how to make a peanut butter and jelly sandwich. Why? Isn't that OK?"

"But doesn't a reader already know that?"

"Yeah. So are you saying that something is missing . . . but what else can you say about this topic?"

When I asked him if he meant the essay to be funny, he said, "Sort of," so I suggested he try to locate and develop the humor in a revision. After he left, I knew that I had been too aggressive in my responses to him and too passive in my readings of his texts. I was not making any effort to read or rather misread meaning or possibility or potential into his writing because I felt convinced that not only was he trying to get away with something, he was provoking and mocking me. Still I was frustrated with myself: rather than calling him on anything directly, saying "I don't want your dredged-up high school essays" or "Why waste your time making fun of the assignment?" I was still concerned with not letting Jack or any of the others know they were getting to me.

It was during the next week that I began to realize why I was so upset by these four students. I also realized I had to confront their resistance more directly while at the same time giving them more room to channel it. So when Jack came back with a revision of the peanut butter and jelly sandwich essay, I responded differently. He had made a few minor changes, but nothing striking. When we discussed it, he said he tried to make it funnier by making the instructions "more ridiculous." When I asked him why he was writing a comic essay on making a peanut butter and jelly sandwich, he had no idea. I suggested that if the essay was meant to be satiric, he ought to think about who or what was being satirized. He seemed totally confused and asked for an example. I said that the essay could, for example, be making fun of technical writers who complicate simple processes. He looked irritated. "Or, maybe you are making fun of teachers who give foolish assignments." He looked surprised for a second, then laughed. I had not planned to confront him in that way, but as soon as I did I was convinced it was the right move.

"I decided to drop the peanut butter and jelly essay," Jack told me in his next conference. "You kept asking me what I learned from writing it and what I wanted the reader to learn and my answer was always 'I don't know, probably nothing.' So I decided that if I couldn't learn anything from it, the reader can't be expected to either. So I wrote an essay about why this wasn't a good topic." Now it could certainly be argued that Jack had simply quit resisting or that he was now putting me on in a new way, but at the time I only focused on how this new essay was an interesting discussion on the role and difficulty of topic selection in the writing process. His main point was that a "simpler topic is actually harder to work with than a more complicated and in-depth one." He tried to prove that point by comparing his peanut butter and jelly essay to a classmate's essay on the death of his father. He argued that he had struggled to generate ideas because his topic was so simple, while his classmate "had many avenues and moral implications to explore." I encouraged him, pointing out that I thought this essay had more potential than his earlier ones. I raised questions about certain nuances of his argument. And I talked a little about what kind of topics I found easier and harder to write about. In short, I finally tried to misread one of his essays in ways that would open up the topic for him and for me. After Jack revised his essay, we both agreed it was by far the strongest piece he had written all semester; not coincidentally, it was also the first one in which we both felt an investment.

Until I recognized that my unconscious responses were creating much of the resistance, Jack stalled as a writer. After that recognition, we both were more productive in our respective roles. The essay on the relative difficulty of certain topics may have begun as the same kind of dare as the first peanut butter and jelly paper, but it is clear that in working on that essay both he and I became interested in the topic, more connected to the text and to each other. In fact, until I could recognize how much my anger and defensiveness were shaping my responses to all four of these student writers, I was not an effective writing teacher for them or for the other students in the class.

The Personal Is Pedagogical

Of course, these four young men may have had difficulty as writers in my class for all sorts of reasons that have nothing to do with my personal hang-ups or limitations. I'm certain there was a combination of explanations for their problems early in the year. But the fact remains that I may have contributed to their problems by responding to them and to their writing in ways that limited our relationship. The same is true in Nicki's case. It's possible that she was able to write effectively in my course partially because of her transference emotions and her identification with me. But it is also true that I may have failed to push her as hard as I might have if I had not been caught up in feeling proud of myself. Nicki's writing directly and indirectly validated my teaching and, as a result, I was flattered; I read the early drafts and behavior of these four males as threatening and critical and, in return, I was defensive and punishing.

There is a sexual component in all this as well: we cannot ignore gender as a factor in the way students respond to their teachers and the way teachers respond to their students. But beyond the sexual tension—most of which is unconscious—there is the simple problem that I respond more favorably to students—male or female—who make me feel secure than to those who threaten me. And that is what I need to monitor: as soon as I find myself giving up on a student or, on the other hand, feeling tremendous personal pride in a student's work, I need to question my own motives. I need to discover in what ways my biases and assumptions—both conscious and uncon-scious—are shaping my teaching.

Now I suspect that this concentration on my own feelings and associations seems self-indulgent and misguided to composition specialists who believe in more "scholarly" research. I further suspect that they would advise me to quit thinking so much about myself and to focus instead on the tropes and conventions of academic discourse, or on the problems of task representation or on new ways to empower student writers. But, as I argued in Chapter 1, these approaches are not mutually exclusive; in fact, I am not sure how we can understand what our students are doing as writers without paying more attention to what we are doing as readers. If we want to find less constrained and constraining ways of responding as writing teachers, we have to examine our responses within the contexts of the relationships in which they occur. By engaging in ongoing self-analysis, by becoming more self-conscious about the source of our misreadings, by recognizing that our unconscious associations are a significant part of a writing course, we can become more creative readers and more effective teachers. By avoiding this process, we will never know in what ways we are limiting our students, their writing, and ourselves.

Chapter Three

Responding to Student Writing (I): Productive Tension in the Writing Conference

It is Michelle's third conference and she looks pleased. "I brought in a revision of that essay about my job at the grocery store. I think I'm about done with it. I think it's better than the last draft. I still might change a few things. I'm not really happy with some of the words I used and stuff. But basically I think it's done. I think I'm going to start on my second essay this week." I read the introduction in silence.

> During the summer I worked in a grocery store as a cashier. This is a great opportunity for anyone who enjoys observing the behavior of people.

Already I feel uncomfortable. This is exactly how her last draft started. Is the point of her "about done" essay that she has observed people shopping?

> In my observations I noticed how many shoppers decide to shop at the same time and at the most awkward hours. The strangest hours are usually the busiest. What is frustrating is that while you are ready to leave for home there is a mad rush for last minute groceries. And customers can become very irritating at times, too.

Now my fears are almost confirmed: this is not the revision that I hinted at last week, that I thought we had agreed she would try to write. How can she feel the essay is done? I glance down the page to her conclusion.

Most customers enjoy a cheerful greeting from a cashier, but when a cashier has been dealing with difficult people all day it is hard to be polite. Working in a grocery store has opened my eyes to the fact that there is not much emphasis on person to person dealings in the business world.

That paragraph sounds vaguely familiar and I remember why: in her last conference, Michelle had brought in a draft organized loosely around her personal observations of shoppers. She had started that conference in a very different way: "I know this isn't really a good topic but I can't think of anything to write about. I never really did this kind of writing in high school." She went on to say that her high school teacher gave her "rules and examples" to follow and that in a way she liked that better. "At least you knew what you had to do." Because she seemed discouraged, self-defeating, and anxious, I tried to build up her confidence, to make her feel that she did have something to write about and the authority to write about it. I asked her why she didn't like her job and she told me about rude customers. I asked her why she thought they behaved that way. She didn't know. I asked her if she was especially sympathetic to cashiers when *she* shopped in grocery stores and she laughed. "No. I'm kind of like the people who come into the store where I work." And so I encouraged her: "You do have things to write about. You're an expert on this subject; you've seen it from both sides. And since everyone has had some of the experiences you describe, readers will recognize your expertise and will want to understand what really goes on. Now what interests *you* about that relationship? What do *you* want to know more about?"

And so in that way I had led Michelle to this decision to look at "person to person dealings," to this attempt to find meaning in her observations. But I had hoped for much more than this. "Let me just look at your introduction again," I mumble, stalling for time, looking at the words on the page but thinking about what I should say. Now how should I respond to this draft? Certainly Michelle seems to feel better about her writing (and better about herself) in this conference. But *I* am feeling worse. I am feeling anxious. I see potential here but it is still basically unrealized and I am not comfortable with her confidence in the essay, with her decision to move on to another draft.

I am tempted just to tell her what is wrong, but I hesitate. I am aware that Michelle and I are not the only ones in this writing conference. Don Murray is here, reminding me that writers need the time and the encouragement to find their voices and their meaning (*Writer* 157). I hear Brannon and Knoblauch's argument about students' rights to their own texts. And I can't stop thinking about Ferguson McKay, whose case studies clearly demonstrate his thesis that "confidence is a writer's central need" (100). But there are other voices in the room as well: Thomas Carnicelli insists that I must accept my "professional obligation" (116) to give my opinion of each student essay; Pamela Richards argues that writers need to hear the truth because "the feeling that someone is humoring me [as a writer] is more damaging to my sense of self than outright attack" (118); and my colleagues, chairperson, dean, former teachers, and conscience all tell me that standards are important, that this draft needs to be revised, that Michelle has not pushed herself hard enough.

I finally speak: "So you are happier with this draft?" A nonquestion. I am still stalling. She has already told me that she is. But I want some time to think and I have learned that getting students to do the talking in these situations is essential. Often, when pushed just a little, students who claim to be finished with a draft will admit that the draft still needs work, that they still have questions and doubts, and, sometimes, that they even know what is wrong and how to fix it. But I have no such luck today.

"Yeah, I am." I wait to see if she will give up anything at all. Finally she asks directly, "Is it OK?" Her tone has changed now; she is sounding much less confident, aware that I am not satisfied.

"Well . . . I definitely see progress from your last one. . . . I am interested in the point about the impersonal environment of the store. Could you tell me more about that?" She doesn't answer; instead she picks up her essay and begins reading as if she hasn't seen it before. "I mean, is that really your central point, that the atmosphere in the store makes people behave in a certain way?"

Damn. Why can't I ever let long silences remain? As soon as I answer one of my own questions, I always remember Graves's point about the value of silence and patience in writing conferences (99), but with a struggling student sitting there I often can't take it. I just keep thinking I have to get them, get us, over these uncomfortable moments. But that's the problem. Am I helping them by talking or helping me?

"I guess I could try to focus more on my point about how the atmosphere of the store makes people—the customers and the cashiers—act a certain way and they don't even realize it."

"Fine. Why don't you try that?"

As Michelle gets up to leave, I worry once again whether I talked too much, too little, or some of each.

Productive Tension in the Writing and Reading Processes

I do not present Michelle's conference as a model for teacher training. In fact, I would argue that there *is* no model or typical conference. Like writing, the writing conference is a process—not static, not a noun, not a thing, but rather active, dynamic, organic. It changes with each student and each teacher and each second, and although there is value (even necessity) in developing a logical theory and approach, we need to learn to work with students to "write" the conference as well as the essay, to learn when our response should dictate the process and when the process should dictate our response.

But while the specifics of Michelle's conference may not be typical, the issues her conference raises are. When and how should we respond to a student's writing? And how should we deal with the tension that writers *and* teachers often feel in writing conferences? In many "first generation" writing conferences (Roger Garrison's early conferences would be an example), teachers answered these questions with a set agenda and direct instruction. They used conference time to solve problems. "Here is what is wrong; here is how you can fix it." But as process replaced product in the classroom, it did so also in the conference, and "second generation" conference teachers (following Murray's lead) focused more on questions than on answers, more on structural issues than on superficial problems. Still, this process approach to conference teaching became ritualized in its own ways: "Always start by offering encouragement." "Focus on only one or two things in each conference." "Do as little of the talking as possible." "Never take over a student's essay."

If we want to understand how writing conferences work (and why some fail), we need to move beyond a set of rigid rules for conference teachers to an approach that takes into account the dynamic aspects of each writing conference: the student's relationship to the text, the teacher's relationship to the text, and the student's and teacher's relationship to each other. To be effective, conference teachers must monitor the tension created within and between these relationships and strive to keep that tension at a productive level—for their students and for themselves.

In this context, the level of tension is "productive" only if it keeps the writing and reading processes alive. When the tension level is too high, writers freeze, panic, resist, retreat (telling themselves either "I really don't have anything to say" or "I have a lot to say but I can't get it down on paper"); when the level is too low, they lack the interest, curiosity, desire, even pain, that compels someone to keep writing effectively. But the students' tension is only half the picture: when the tension level is too high (i.e., when teachers fear that their students are not making progress or lack the skills to produce a successful essay), teachers also panic and retreat (reverting to "objective" assignments, frequent grading, direct instruction); when the level is too low, they lack the curiosity and desire that compels someone to keep reading and responding effectively. For the writing conference to work, the teacher must establish a level of tension that is productive not only for the student but also for herself.

I do not mean to suggest here that tension is an end in itself; rather I am suggesting that we focus on tension—our students' and our own—because it will help us make practical decisions about when and how to intervene in any individual conference. Guided by valuable research (such as Mike Rose's study of writer's block or Susan McLeod's examination of the significance of affective factors in a student's writing process), most conference teachers already consider a student's attitude when making those decisions. When a student seems tense, stuck, frustrated, we encourage, support, and question; when a student seems self-satisfied, refusing to go beyond his first superficial responses to a complex topic (probably because he is tense, stuck, frustrated), we push, provoke, and question. But what about when we are feeling self-satisfied or stuck or tense? Whether we are aware of it or not, our expectations, frustrations, and associations, our responses and nonresponses, also shape the student's level of tension, the dynamics of the conference, and the direction of the subsequent revision.

But these two levels of tension—the student's and the teacher's—are interrelated not only because they each change in response to the other, but also because the frustration and tension that a teacher experiences in a writing conference is similar to the frustration and tension that a writer experiences. There are no clear right or wrong answers for conference writers or for conference teachers, and each must learn the same lessons: to experiment, to take risks, to follow seemingly random associations, and to be suspicious of quick fixes. Neither writers nor writing teachers know exactly how much tension they need or can tolerate at any one time; what counts is that a student and teacher have enough confidence in each other and in themselves to keep the process going. The trick is in negotiating the tension so that the student and teacher believe not only that the student has the potential to achieve her goals in the essay but also that those goals are worth achieving.

Unfortunately, teachers in both the product and the process camps seem to fear tension and often try hard to reduce or eliminate it. These teachers have good intentions: they know that many students have been traumatized by writing and writing teachers and they also know (as Rose's research has demonstrated) that too much tension is debilitating, even paralyzing for a writer. But while we can decrease tension in certain areas of the process, we cannot (and should not try to) make writing or teaching writing entirely painless. We should not strive to make everyone in the writing class "as comfortable as possible," a goal appropriate for terminally ill patients but not for teachers and writers. Rather than wasting time trying to dissipate tension, we need to expend more energy finding ways to use that tension in productive ways. In the final analysis, we can do that only by carefully studying our students and ourselves.

In the following case studies, I have tried to look carefully at the role tension played in my students' draft writing and my conference teaching and to understand how that tension shaped our relationship and each subsequent revision. These case studies reveal at least as much about me as a conference teacher as they reveal about each of these student writers. They reveal, for example, my tendencies to offer editorial (and sometimes extremely directive) comments as if they were questions, to push students to write introspective, almost confessional essays, and most of all to try to sustain a relatively high level of tension in each conference.

One way I try to control the tension is to keep things—issues, essays, ideas—relatively unresolved. I ask students to "finish" only three essays in fifteen weeks. No topics are assigned. No drafts are graded. The guidelines are intentionally open-ended: usually I ask students to write one personal narrative, one argument or analysis of a written work, and one essay analyzing some aspect of their own writing process. During the semester each student has a weekly conference in which he or she is expected to bring an essay to discuss (either a new draft or a revision). Generally students work for five or six weeks on a draft and then move on to another.

Regarding the following case- (or self-)studies, I first recorded my immediate response to each conference (labeled here as "Postconference Response"). In this response (which is similar in method and purpose to a writer's protocol analysis), I tried to show what I was thinking and feeling during and immediately after the conference. The "Analysis" sections were written after the semester ended.

Tension in the Writing Conference: Two Case Studies

Case Study 1: Denise

Conference 1

I read Denise's draft while she sits quietly. Her thesis: "I never knew that there were so many preparations that go into getting ready for a wedding. But now that my sister is getting married next month I am getting a chance to see how much work is really involved." From there she goes on to list everything—ordering flowers, sending out invitations, etc. I am struck by one section of the paper: "I am not sure why, but I am not really that excited about the wedding yet. I keep getting this kind of empty feeling. I am sure I will be excited, though, when the event comes." But then she returns to a list of the preparations. She ends the draft by stating that in spite of all the work involved she still believes in marriage.

In the middle of the conference, she says that she is "sort of happy" with the essay but that she "feels stuck" about how to revise it.

"Well, what interests you most in this essay?"

"I don't know."

"Did anything surprise you in writing this?"

"Not really."

"Did you learn anything new about weddings or about how you feel about this one?"

"Not really. What do you mean?"

"Well what about this paragraph about the empty feeling?" Long pause. "It seems different to me. Does it to you?"

"Well it is about feelings, and the rest is just a list of facts."

"Yes. Do you want to write more about that?"

"I guess so. It's just that there is so much to do for a wedding. There's like ten showers, and when I was home last week I had to spend almost an entire day doing stuff for the shower we're giving. I didn't really mind but I was just home for two days."

"So will you write more on this?"

"I don't know. What interests you most?"

"That paragraph because it is different, like you said. There is more tension there, more unanswered questions, don't you think?"

"So maybe I should write more about that?"

"I think so, but I don't want to be pushy. It's your essay, not mine."

"No. I need the help, the advice. In high school I never had to write this kind of paper before. We always got assigned topics about books and we always wrote five-paragraph essays. I don't know how to do this."

Postconference Response

As usual, I feel good about some parts, bad about others. Again I see an essay here before she does and it is better than what she has and I can tell that she does not see it herself. So I directed her attention to it. But that's all. I didn't interpret it, though I do have an interpretation: she is jealous of her sister and all the attention she is getting. That is what I think she really feels. And I am thinking that she could write a great essay about how weddings and other big events are supposed to make us feel good but often they don't because we all bring our own emotional baggage: "Did you ever wonder why so many people cry at weddings?" That is how I would start it. But it isn't my essay. I know she needs to get the details down on paper, write her way through that phase before she can or dares to shape it, to interpret it. Experience with students writing about painful experiences—like the death of a family member, the breakup of a friendship—has taught me that. Give her time to find her point. Am I directing too much already? I need to be patient. I need to shut up. But I also need to reassure her (and me) that teaching and learning are going on here.

Conference 2

In her next draft, she explores her feelings of ambivalence. She does raise the question of jealousy over all the attention her sister is receiving. But, she says, her "empty feeling" isn't caused by jealousy: "I will get my turn to have a big wedding someday." Then she raises the question of worry for her sister, but she says it couldn't be that either because "I like my sister's fiancé. I know he will be good for her." She concludes that her emptiness is probably nothing significant. "I can't wait till it is over, though, so we can get back to normal."

In the conference she expresses frustration again with the revision process. I keep pushing her, hoping she will decide to take up the problem of her ambivalence. Finally, I ask directly about her negative feelings.

"I don't know. I'm not sure what it is. I mean I am excited about the wedding but there is something . . ." I hesitate. She says nothing. The she shrugs and laughs nervously. "I really don't know."

I hesitate again. Finally I speak up: "Maybe before you revise it next time you should just write down ideas and feelings you associate with the empty feeling. You know, just list anything that comes to mind. Want to try that?"

Postconference Response

God, I am feeling lousy about this. She just doesn't seem to get this "sight into insight" idea (Annie Dillard's description of writing) and maybe I just need to show her what I mean. There is a good paper here about jealousy, about feeling lousy when you are supposed to feel happy. But if I tell her that is the paper then she is not writing the paper in the sense that writing is thinking and seeing. I am making the breakthrough. Again I have to remember Murray's advice about patience and faith. Faith that the student on her own will find her own meaning and that that meaning will be worth finding. And I don't know if she is capable of it.

Conference 3

In the next conference she brings in her revision, in which she again runs through all the stuff that can't be causing her "empty feeling" and then says, "First there was my parents' divorce two years ago and then I went away to college and now my sister won't even have the same last name. Sometimes I wish that I could be back in middle school when our whole family was living together under one roof." So, she suggests, "Maybe my sadness is because the wedding is the last step in my nuclear family splitting apart." Still she concludes by stating, "I still am excited for my sister and still look forward to the day that I am walking down the aisle."

I am immediately struck by how much stronger this draft is. In fact, when I read that paragraph about her family's disintegrations and how that made her feel, I experience as a reader the kind of "felt sense" that Sondra Perl associates with writers when they discover their meaning and voice and purpose. Denise seems to feel better about it but she is not sure why or what to do next. I want her to keep working on this draft, to focus and organize her ideas more effectively, but I also want her to leave knowing what she has accomplished. And so after some discussion of specific aspects of her revision, I ask her: "This is a much stronger draft, don't you think?"

"Yeah. I do."

"Do you see how this thesis—about why you have that empty feeling—is a different kind of thesis than your other ones?"

"Yeah. It's more about why I feel that way. Before I just had a lot of facts. Now I think I have more of a point."

Postconference Response

That was a great conference. Or a great essay. Or both. I was so sure about the jealousy issue and so smug about that. And worried that I would have to tell her in the end. "Look. Write this." And then she comes in and writes this essay that is so much better, that really goes much further with the topic in a way that shows her thinking, not mine. Well maybe it shows my way of thinking, my bias towards introspective, epiphany essays. But the epiphany itself came from her, not from me.

Conference 4

She brings in a revision with a few minor editing changes, no substantial changes. I ask her if she plans to keep working on this essay and she says, "No, I want to start on my second one." So we discuss her ideas for her new essay.

Postconference Response

In some ways I am a little disappointed. The essay took such a leap last week that I hoped it would just keep getting deeper and deeper and better and better. Also, I hoped she would pick up on that stuff about her own fear of marriage. I figured I had it all figured out. She put that part in about her own marriage even before she knew why because unconsciously her fear is that her own marriage could never work out because her parents' marriage did not. She did not pursue that, she said, because her paper is now not about that topic. And she is right. I have to quit writing another paper in my head. No that isn't it. I have to write many different papers. I have to make connections and I have to ask students, carefully, nondramatically, if my connections make sense to them. Of course this essay could go further but I don't think she can right now. And I have to be grateful for what she has gotten out of this material, not regretful about what she has missed.

Analysis

This study demonstrates my belief that the associations of writing teachers have to play a crucial role in the writing conference. When I read Denise's line about the empty feeling, I sensed that it was the real center of her essay. Now I had several options: I could have kept my sense to myself, letting her find her own focus and question; conversely, I could have told her directly that I wanted her to write her essay on that sentence and then offered my own interpretation of her feelings; or I could have taken a middle path, asking questions in which I was truly interested but trusting her to find her own meaning. Of course, in retrospect I am glad I took that middle path. By finding the sentence that contained the most (the only?) real tension in her essay, I played a role in the process. But in that role I was never trying to take over the essay; I was just trying to keep the ball in her court.

And in this case that "worked." But I have participated in enough writing conferences to know this rarely happens so neatly. Since the path leading from a teacher's unconscious associations to a student's essay is long, winding, and unclearly marked, most of these associations fail to find their way into print. In the same semester that Denise wrote this essay, many of my other students rejected, failed to recognize, or radically transformed my associations and clues. Is this a good thing or a bad one? It is impossible to say, since we have no way of knowing what sort of essay a student would have written without listening to a teacher's suggestions or associations or what part of the credit for a successful draft is due to a teacher's suggestions. It makes sense, I think, to follow the (slightly altered) advice of Hawthorne's famous narrator: "Be true! Be true! Be true! Show freely to your [students] if not your worst fear [and your greatest hope] for their [writing], yet some trait whereby the worst [and best] may be inferred!" (*Scarlet Letter* 183). That way we give students enough help to keep them going, but not so much that we cut off their options.

Case Study 2: Evan

Conference 1

His essay is about a fight he had with his best friend in high school. The fight began with a practical joke. His friend had hidden Evan's car keys and would not tell him where they were. Evan "got back at the friend" the next day by placing several fire crackers in his friend's car. They created "a lot of noise and smoke but no damage or anything." The friend retaliated immediately by ripping the side mirror off Evan's car. The paper has no conclusion or analysis.

"I'm not really happy with this draft." That is how he starts the conference.

"Why not?"

"It has too many details . . . don't you think? And I didn't stick to my topic. My title is too general, too."

"You describe this fight clearly."

"Yeah I think that's the strongest part."

"I do too. Do you think you will keep working on this one?"

"No."

"Why not?"

"It's too personal."

"Would writing help you gain perspective on it, understand it better?"

"I have perspective on it already. It's just personal."

"OK. That's fine. It is up to you to decide which essays you want to revise."

We then discuss some of his other paper ideas.

Postconference Response

I'm frustrated in some ways. His essay is ragged—all of the problems with mechanics—but it has potential. He seems very upset, clearly resistant to pursuing this topic. Which naturally makes me more interested in it. I see the potential because I like essays that start with conflict, confusion, questions. No, that's not true; I like essays that start with order, a superficial order, and then unravel into conflict, confusion, questions, and then get put back together again in a new, better order. Evan cares about this fight but (or so) he cannot yet make sense of it. It is too painful for him to pursue. I felt dumb, embarrassed, asking him about gaining perspective through writing. He says he has it (I don't think he does) and that makes me feel as if I were prying into his private life, makes me feel a bit like a voyeur. Anyway, I think there is a paper in this experience but unless he thinks there is a paper there, I have to let it go.

Conferences 2–4

Evan spends the next three conferences and drafts on another essay on volunteer firefighters. The essay has no real focus, no real voice. I question him. "Are you saying . . . ?" "Do you want to look at . . . ?" The drafts change a little but still no real focus emerges.

Postconference Responses

I am worried that we are both growing frustrated and will soon lose all confidence in each other's abilities. I'm disappointed that Evan has chosen to pursue this essay rather than the one about the fight. All I know now is that he needs some success soon or he will give up on himself and (I hate to admit this) I will give up on him.

Conference 5

To my great surprise, Evan brings in a revision of the essay about his friend. "Remember that paper I wrote about my fight with my friend. I decided to write another draft about it. I changed it a lot." He has dropped almost the entire narrative section about the details of the fight, leaving only a few sentences from the first essay. Now he starts with a question: "Would a real friend do something terrible to another friend?" He goes on to argue that a real friend would not have torn off his car mirror. He explains again that the firecrackers were harmless. But then he says the funny part is that when his parents asked him what happened to the car, he said, "It was vandalized." Evan concludes the draft this way: "I was still protecting my friend. I think inside he knows what he did was wrong."

"You have cut out a lot of details about the fight itself, haven't you?"

"Yeah I didn't really need them. I wanted to explain more about how I feel."

"Are you happier with this one?"

"Yeah. It's more what I want to say, I think."

"How so?"

"I mean I explained about how I protected him. I told my parents the car was vandalized. That's weird in a way."

"But you say at the end your relationship will never be the same."

"Yeah. I can't forget about it."

"So it's forgiven but not forgotten?"

"Yeah I guess."

"Is that your central point?"

"I'm not sure."

"Isn't that it? You are going beyond the cliché—forgive and forget—to make an important distinction—that it is possible to forgive someone, at least to stop actively fighting with the person, without forgetting the pain of the experience." No response for about twenty seconds. We both stare at the essay. "Actually you have already made this distinction. Look at this first page. It is all about forgiving him, about not telling your parents, about feeling bad about what happened. But then the second page is about how your friendship was never the same after that."

"Uh-uh." No further response for about fifteen seconds.

"Could you start with the cliché, then introduce this idea—that the cliché does not really explain what often happens after an upsetting fight with a friend—and then make your point by explaining how forgiving and forgetting are two very different kind of actions?"

"Uh, yeah."

"And then what?" There is a slight hesitation, and then I speak again: "Do you think you could revise it in that way? How does that sound?"

Postconference Response

All in all I think that was a good conference. I know I talked too much. I know I took over toward the end, but what choice did I have at this point? At least he tried this topic again. The fact that it took him so long to come back to it and the fact that he is still clearly upset about this fight prove that he has finally found a topic that means something to him. And I am glad he moved away from straight narrative to some attempt at analysis, even if he doesn't know yet what he thinks about this stuff. I like the fact that he got into this forgive-and-forget stuff. That is qualitatively better than anything else he has come up with so far. It is about discrimination, questioning, not just describing. But I am afraid I am making it my essay. He seemed not able to recognize his own thesis, his own idea. To him, it was an offhand remark. He offered it almost metaphorically, "You know how people say, 'forgive and forget.' It's kind of like that, except I can forgive him but I can't really forget about it." So I jump on it and ask him about it and still he doesn't quite get it so I keep questioning him and finally I have to almost tell him, "Here is your main point." Could he have reached a different thesis—a better one—without my taking over? I think I made the right decision.

Conference 6

In this draft he has "incorporated" the forgive-and-forget point by stapling a brief handwritten introduction and conclusion to his previous typed draft. Then he has indicated with arrows and numbers on his typed page that I should refer to those handwritten sections. His introduction reads: "In the case of my friendship with my former best friend, the friendship had the quality to forgive but not to forget. Does that change a friendship? In this case it has." As the conclusion he has added: "People always say to forgive and forget is the best thing to retain a friendship. The forgiving part seems to be the easy part. It is the forgetting that's always the hardest. How can I look at him every time and not remember what he did to my car? I'll always remember. I think he knows as well as I do who was in the wrong."

At the end of the conference, Evan comments, "I think I am getting the hang of things now. The conferences help. I get to see what you want, what you think, and then I can make the changes. I am getting to know what you like."

"Is it what I like? Are *you* happy with the revisions?"

"Oh, yeah. Definitely."

Postconference Response

I am not happy with the revisions. The fact that they are just tacked on (literally) to the essay is an indication that they have not made an impression on Evan's thinking. But he is happy. He sensed correctly that I liked the forgive-and-forget idea and now that he has added them he feels better and he is feeling confident. I feel conflicted. I am glad he is finally feeling good about something in his writing, but he is feeling good about something *I* wrote. It's as if I lent something valuable to him and he is grateful and proud. And at first I felt good, too, that I have made him feel better and that I helped our relationship. But now there is a problem: I was just lending him something to try out, to see if he wanted to get one of his own, but he has mistaken it for a gift. So now what do I do? Ask for it back? Give him credit for it? What the hell do I do now?

Conference 7

Evan brings in essentially the same essay, still not effectively integrating his ideas and mine. His attitude, though, is even more positive. "I am feeling much better about my writing now. I have a lot more ideas about how to organize stuff. I don't just throw it down on paper. At the beginning of the year I really didn't know what kind of writing you liked."

Postconference Response

Now I *know* I went too far by suggesting that forgive-and-forget thesis. He never made that point purely his own, but he believes his writing is better, and that has certain advantages. I have tried to encourage him but also to push him to try to write and think on his own. The fact that he still keeps talking about what I want is discouraging and I have contributed to it by telling him too much, by losing confidence in his ability. But again, what was my alternative?

Analysis

Perhaps the most interesting issue here is the role my tension played first in the conferences and then in my postconference comments. Although I admitted that I "took over" Evan's sixth conference "toward the end," I was not aware (until listening to tapes) that I distorted the conferences in my responses so that I could let myself believe I was not in *complete* control of Evan's essay. In retrospect I understand my motivation: I had seen several drafts and had several conferences with Evan and I was growing increasingly worried that the "writing to learn" model was not well suited to his particular skills and needs, that he needed help I was not providing, and that without intervention his essay would stagnate and our relationship would deteriorate. Given these fears, I began to worry that Evan would be unable to flourish within this approach and that I could at least give him some survival skills and some organizational strategies. It was as if I were saying, "Let's forget this meaning and voice stuff. Here is how you write a competent essay."

My perception that Evan was not making progress and that we were both ready to give up dictated my aggressive response. When I listened to the tapes, I found that the first statement of the forgive-and-forget idea actually came from me and not from Evan (as I reported in my response). I made myself think that *he* suggested it because that helped me feel less anxious about taking over his essay.

For me the key is what I wrote after his fourth conference: "He needs some success soon or he will give up on himself and (I hate to admit this) I will give up on him." To keep the process going, I needed to provide a great deal of structure, so much that I no longer viewed the draft as his. Once I felt compelled to offer Evan such direct advice about the thesis and organization of the essay, I was admitting unconsciously that the process had broken down. I was unwilling to let him (or me) continue to struggle and so I tried to cut my losses by giving Evan some sense of accomplishment and confidence in the hope that we would both do better on his next draft. The fact that I did not fully admit this to myself makes sense to me in retrospect: I was trying to control my own tension; I was trying to find a way to help both of us stay with the process.

Beyond Good Conference Teacher/ Bad Conference Teacher

I hope these case studies reflect some of the tension of real writing conferences and suggest the need for a decision-making process that goes beyond prescriptive rules to an emphasis on interpersonal relationships. And on the conscious and unconscious associations the student and teacher bring to each text and each conference. While it is convenient to identify a particular style of conference teaching as either "student based" or "teacher based," such neat categories fail to reflect the messily collaborative nature of conference teaching.

I felt frustrated by the inadequacy of this either-or approach as soon as I started using conferences to teach writing, but I did not know that others felt the same frustration until I participated in a workshop a few years ago on the teacher's role in writing conferences. To demonstrate the different styles and strategies available to teachers, the workshop leaders gave us two packs of handouts. They were each transcripts of writing conferences. In the first ones, the teachers interrupted, badgered, lectured, and trampled over their students, ending conferences by telling the student what to write for the next draft and how to write it. The second group of teachers asked questions, murmured "Mm" and "Yes, I see" at appropriate times, and encouraged enthusiastic students' plans for revision. The leaders then analyzed this good teacher/bad teacher exercise: "We can believe in freedom or authority; we can let our students write their own papers or we can take over their essays and make them our own."

But in the question-and-answer period, a teacher, looking and sounding exasperated, spoke up. "Of course, I wouldn't treat my students like those first teachers did, but my conferences hardly ever turn out like the second ones either. For me the question is what I can do to help my students learn to write. I have a student who is taking comp for the third time because he keeps failing our college's proficiency exam and he comes to conferences trying to improve and I try to let him lead the way, to let him control our conferences. I keep waiting for him to figure out how to improve his own writing. But it is not happening. And when he is struggling with the organization of one of his essays, I can hardly stand it any longer. It takes all of my energy to keep myself from grabbing his pen and his paper out of his hand, writing down an outline, and yelling, 'Look, it goes *this* way!' I want to know how to deal with *that*."

Now there must be teachers like the ones in the handouts, but I don't feel I have much in common with them. It is the teacher who spoke up at the end of that workshop who stays with me in writing conferences and in my research. I know what he is feeling. After all, I've been there myself.

Chapter Four

Responding to Student Writing (II): What We Really Think About When We Think About Grades

My brother and I started teaching the same year in the same city—he at an open admissions university in downtown Chicago, I at a high school on the southwest side. There is one incident that stands out in my mind from our first semesters of teaching: I stopped by Joe's apartment one afternoon to find him pacing the floor. He had spent the whole morning reading the essay answers on the final exam he had given the day before, and one of his students, a thirty-year-old Nigerian student named John Nmtembo, had written him a note across the top of the first page: "Please Mr. Tobin. I need an A. I want to be a doctor when I go back to Nigeria. But first I need A on exam and A on course."

Joe was in a panic. He had read the first page, he said, and it was fine, competent, but definitely not an A. But there, at the bottom of the page was another note. "Please Mr. Tobin. A. A. Must have A." And so with a sense of doom, Joe headed on to page two. But like Poe's Raven, John Nmtembo's words awaited him there, too. "Please, please, please. A! A! A!" By the end of the last page, John's exam answers had grown more concise and perfunctory, while his pleas, demands, and chants had virtually taken over the margins:

A, Mr. Tobin, A!
A, Mr. Tobin, A!
Must, must, must get A, A, A!
A, Mr. Tobin, A!

By the time I arrived, Joe had reread the exam three times. He looked sick. "What am I going to do? There is no way in the world that this is an A. To tell you the truth, I'm not even sure that it's a B."

I hadn't yet given out my first set of grades, but I knew a nightmare when I heard one: "So what are you going to do?"

"I don't know. I can't give him an A. It's just not right. But I can't give him a C, either. When he goes back to Nigeria, he wants to be a doctor? I can't give him a C. He'd have a breakdown."

"When do you have to turn in grades?"

"Not till next week. But that's not the worst part. Look at this."

And there on the bottom of John Nmtembo's exam was a final note: "Mr. Tobin, please you *must* call me today as soon as you read this exam. I need A and will wait at my apartment for your call. Please Mr. Tobin!" And so like a man headed for a sentencing after the jury has already declared him guilty, he trudged into his den to call John with the news.

Waiting in the living room, I thought about how much I hated giving grades and about how glad I was that I didn't have to break the news to John Nmtembo. But when Joe came back from the den, he looked more stunned than upset. "What happened?"

"It was unbelievable." He answered and I said, "John, this is Joe Tobin. I just finished grading your exam and I'm afraid I have some disappointing news for you. You wrote a lot of good answers and it is a solid exam but I just don't think there is enough there to warrant an A. I'm afraid that I'm going to have to give you a B." And then *he* says, "You give me a B!? Thank you, Mr. Tobin, thank you, a B? Thank you!"

Although the story of John Nmtembo may not seem like beauty or truth, I think of it as my Grecian urn on grading; in my most cynical moments I think it is all I know about assessment and all I need to know. Assessment is never objective or clean; it is never easily and painlessly resolved. Not all interactions with students are quite as charged and dramatic as the one between my brother and John Nmtembo, but the same issues of power, resistance, seduction, and manipulation are always present in some form. In other words, grading never occurs outside the complicated issues of interpersonal relationships, and academic writing never occurs outside the complicated issues of grading. The key is not to look for an easy and painless method of assessment, but rather to examine the ways in which grades operate in our teaching and then to ask, what can we do to limit the potentially negative influence of grades on the writing process and on the teacher-student relationship?

Mystery, Subjectivity, and Bias: The Truth About Grades

Most writing teachers hate grading—and for good reason. No matter how much we want to talk about writing as a process, as a mode of thinking and discovery and experimentation, grades remind us and our students that there is always a bottom line. And although most of us have reconciled ourselves to this in a general sense, each time we confront a specific decision—each time we need to decide between an A- and a B+, each time we have to give a C to an essay about a grandparent's death—most of us suffer and wince.

The problem, as Peter Elbow ("Embracing") and others have described it, is that our role as graders seems to run counter to our role as teachers. What's wrong with this picture? A teacher—let's say it's me—spends months telling his students that essays are never really finished (it's just that deadlines arrive); that the writing process is dynamic, recursive, nonlinear, and nonstandard; that reading and interpretation, like writing, are productive acts; that different teachers like different kinds of essays better and worse than others; that writing can be a way for people not only to convey what they already know about themselves and the world but also to come to know those things in the first place; that writing can be creative, liberating, empowering, surprising, therapeutic, and cathartic. Then he takes out a computer printout marked "Freshman English" and writes down a neat little row of numerals: C+, A-, D, B, B+ . . .

Typically, most process teachers argue that we need to reassess assessment; we need, according to most standard thinking, to implement two fundamental changes: we need to make grades less important and, at the same time, we need to make grades more understandable, objective, and fair. But while these are both noble goals, they are both in some sense naive and misleading—and, as far as I can tell, neither one will lead to more productive writing relationships. Let me explain.

Why we can't make grades less important

While my first temptation was to avoid writing about assessment (just as my temptation is to avoid giving grades in the first place), it is one problem that just won't be avoided (or so my students, my department chairman, and my editor remind me). As much as we in the process movement want to move the conversation away from grades, as much as we want to move assessment into the background so that our students can focus on the process of writing, we need to recognize the futility of that wish. The tension around evaluation is at the center of everything I have talked about so far. When Steve wrote that provocative essay about the Jewish reporter, when Nicki criticized her humanities professor's rigid criteria for assessment, when Denise initially resisted my suggestion that she revise her essay, they were testing me and themselves and the system. (I talk more about how important grades are to students—even or especially in writing classes that try to deemphasize competition—in Chapter 6.)

But this consciousness about assessment is not limited to students: when I read a student essay, when I talk with students about composing, when I respond in a conference, I am almost always aware that grades are present; they are the elephants I am trying unsuccessfully not to think about. It seems relatively unproductive, then, to ask whether grades are bad or good (significantly, I originally typed "god" here by mistake) or what student writing would be without them. Grades are currently an integrated, even central, part not only of our academic institutions but also of our entire society. I am not only talking about the literal power of grades—the fact that they are used to determine class rank and scholarships and graduate school admissions; I'm also talking about their tremendous psychic power, about the way they shape a student's self-image and self-esteem.

What would our classrooms be like without grades? For most of us, it makes as much sense to ask, what would our culture be like without money? Grades are a currency that we, as teachers, carry into our classrooms and that our students can earn, save, and spend; they are, in other words, both a cause and an effect of a student's performance and a teacher's power. And like competition, anger, and tension, the struggle for power and the desire for approval and reward need to be acknowledged and controlled or, ultimately, they will control us.

Why we can't make grades understandable, objective, and fair

I recognize, of course, that it seems a bit perverse to argue against such a reasonable and humane goal as "make grading fair and objective"; we have all been schooled in a system that tells us our own attitudes and tastes should not be part of the process, that we should willingly suspend all belief when we grade. As a result, it has become second nature for us to tell our students, our colleagues, and ourselves that we are being objective and fair graders. But how is that possible? The grades we give to essays can never really be fully understandable, objective, or fair, for there is always a degree of mystery, subjectivity, and bias in our response to a written text. As I argue in Chapter 2, I come to this position in part from literary theory and from the belief that no text has an inherent and fixed meaning, let alone an inherent and fixed value. But my teaching experience has taught me the same thing—that writing and reading always involve interpersonal interaction between two or more people. To pretend that we can "objectively" assess the writer (much less the writing) without paying equal attention to the role we play as the reader is, I think, naive.

Someone may argue that if this is a question of degree, why not strive to make grades as understandable, fair, and objective *as possible under the circumstances*? Here, too, I am somewhat hesitant because in order to make grades more understandable, fair, and objective we must make our criteria and expectations less sophisticated, subtle, and dynamic. In other words, the more we limit our definition of what writing is and what constitutes good writing, the easier it is to be "understandable, objective, and fair": but at the same time, the more we limit our definition of what writing is and what constitutes good writing, the harder it is to do justice to the complexity and richness of what really happens when we read and write. Assessment can be made more "objective" only in inverse ratio to the complexity of our definition of writing. Grading becomes "objective" for teachers who have decided that the teaching of writing is "objective."

"What's the big deal?" one of my colleagues asked at our recent department meeting about the problem of assessment in Freshman Comp. She said she has absolutely no problems grading essays and students. She has no problem distinguishing an A from a B or a B from a C. But she didn't stop here; she went on to explain, significantly I think, that she finds the entire business of teaching writing to be straightforward and easy:

> How hard can it be to teach writing? We all know that good essays are made up of good paragraphs and good paragraphs are made up of good sentences. And we all should know what makes a good sentence, right? We're all English teachers. I would hope that we all can recognize a split infinitive or a dangling modifier when we see one.

And I would hope that we all can recognize someone who has spent much more time scanning the lines of *Beowulf* than actually trying to teach students to write (under the circumstances, it took all of my self-discipline not to place "actually" in the middle of "to teach" in that sentence). But as naive as this teacher's position sounds, it raises a crucial question that we must answer before we can evaluate anything: what are we teaching, anyway? Just what *is* writing instruction?

And maybe that's the one good thing about assessment and all this talk about fairness and objectivity: it forces us (or at least it *should* force us) to define our own goals and values. Is a composition class about products or process, about skills, strategies, or attitudes? Is it a preparation for other courses or a course with its own autonomous agenda and integrity? How we answer these questions should determine our approach to grading. If, to take one position, the primary goal of a writing course is to teach students to follow the rules outlined in Strunk and White's *The Elements of Style,* then that will dictate one kind of grading method; if, to take a very different position, the primary goal is to make students want to use writing to clarify their own values and sense of self, then that will lead to a very different method of assessment. Or, to introduce still another alternative, if our primary goal is to prepare students to produce successful academic discourse in lab reports, term papers, essay exams, and so on, then that will lead to still another grading system. My point is fairly obvious: assessment and curriculum are always inseparably linked and we can't (or shouldn't) alter one without altering the other.

Of course, we would hope that the goals of the curriculum would precede and dictate the methods of assessment, but I suspect that it is often the other way around; in many courses, departments, and schools, assessment drives curriculum. In fact, radical educator Jerry Farber argues that grading "is not merely essential to the system; in a way, it is the system" (135). I suppose this should not be surprising. Teaching is difficult enough without all the stress associated with grading. So if there is a way to "teach to the test," it is unfortunately a tempting choice for many teachers and students. Of course, in order to do this in composition courses, a teacher needs to develop an extremely narrow definition of writing and extremely limited goals for his students. In other words, a teacher can do this only by deciding that composition is the acquisition of a specific body of knowledge. This decision then makes it possible to grade students as they are graded in many courses—based on their performances on "objective" exams. We could, for example, give them tests that simply ask them to follow straightforward directions:

- Name the three types of compare and contrast essays.

- Write a sentence that contains a subordinate clause.

- Explain the function of a paragraph.

- Summarize Aristotle's definition of "ethos."

Perhaps I am setting up a straw man or woman here; perhaps there are very few composition teachers who would still be satisfied with such a narrow goal for a writing course. I assume that most teachers would argue that their students need to learn more than a specific set of facts; they need to learn to write by writing.

Still, what does it mean to learn to write? If it means to acquire a specific set of strategies, heuristics, and sentence structures, then grading may still be relatively understandable, objective, and fair. We could develop a carefully defined system of skills and rewards that we could then distribute and explain to students in an effort to minimize confusion and disagreement about grades. Irwin Hashimoto's example in *Thirteen Weeks* is as good as any other: for each particular assignment, he spells out in advance the particular errors or omissions for which he will deduct points—say, seven points for each spelling error, five points for each unclear or "fuzzy" sentence, two points for a weak or useless title, and so on. At the same time he also tells them they cannot lose points on that assignment for other problems or oversights. This, he argues, eliminates much of the uncertainty, arbitrariness, and unfairness of less clearly delineated grading systems.

But while this certainly makes grading easier, I'm not convinced it can be implemented without oversimplifying the processes of reading and writing. I suppose it could work effectively if we taught writing as a mechanistic process. We could, for example, tell students to write a five-paragraph essay with the thesis statement at the end of the first paragraph. We could tell them that they must support this thesis statement with three supporting points and then support each of those points with three specific examples, statistics, or facts. And we could say that there should be a clear and effective transition that links each new paragraph with the previous one and a conclusion that summarizes without simply restating. We could then assign a specific number of points to each of these parts (twenty points for the thesis, five points for each transition, etc.) and explain as specifically as possible what would earn the maximum points in each category (e.g., "A twenty-point thesis statement is clear, concise, and original").

So what's wrong with this solution? First, we would still find ourselves in frequent disagreements with our students about whether a title is or is not weak, whether a transition is or is not effective. So instead of arguing with students over one overall grade, we now must argue over dozens of small grades (Is this thesis worth sixteen points or seventeen? Is this a three- or a four-point transition?). While Hashimoto welcomes this sort of process, suggesting that our assessments should be "always negotiable," I have found this sort of microhaggling to be unproductive for me as a reader, for the student as a writer, and most of all for our relationship.

Second, and more importantly, this approach fails to recognize the complexity and richness of reading and writing. Words, sentences, paragraphs, essays, students, and teachers do not exist in decontextualized isolation, and learning to write is not merely learning to follow directions or recipes. While I do not deny the importance of learning the conventions of argument, grammar, usage, documentation, and so on, a writing course is also about writing to discover values, to recover memories, and to uncover easy assumptions and prejudices. Given these more dynamic and admittedly ambitious goals, the efforts to reduce and restrict writing to something that can be more easily assessed are simply wrongheaded and weak-kneed.

Let me put it another way: while it may be tempting to reduce writing to prescriptive definitions, this sort of reduction will inevitably lead to a "murder to dissect" system of reading, responding, and assessing. As Thoreau suggested, once you shoot an eagle out of the sky, cut it up on the operating table, and point out where it gets its tremendous power and grace, it doesn't seem all that powerful and graceful anymore—or even worth looking at in the first place.

But it is not simply the power and complexity of writing that defy objectivity; it is also the context in which academic reading and writing occur—the context of interpersonal relationships. The truth is that all assessment occurs within and is heavily shaped by complex interpersonal relationships that simply are not completely understandable, objective, or fair. As readers, we are necessarily biased, idiosyncratic, culturally situated, and quirky. Don't our grades necessarily reflect something of our own training, temperament, politics, and values? And, even more, don't we evaluate each piece of student writing by taking into account all sorts of subtle, nuanced aspects of the particular teacher-student relationship that produced it?

To answer this question I decided to watch myself read—in other words, to do a reading protocol of myself. While I read and graded some student essays from one of my first-year writing courses, I recorded my thoughts and concerns. Now, of course, most of my thoughts were "content based," such as "Great sentence" or "I don't get it. Are you saying . . . ?" or "Where's your evidence?" But many others were "relationship based" and, in fact, had little or nothing to do with the actual words on the page in front of me. As a result of this unofficial experiment (which, by the way, I highly recommend) I complied the following list:

Thirteen things that I think about when I give grades
that teachers are not supposed to think about when
we give grades:

1. What grade does this student expect? Or a related question: what grade is she secretly hoping for?

2. How will this student feel when he hears this grade? Will he feel happy? angry? disappointed? surprised?

3. What action might this student take as a result of this grade? Is she likely to complain? to me? to her classmates? to the department chairperson?

4. How might other students respond to this grade? Will they hear that I gave so-and-so an A and say, "I knew that she was the teacher's pet"? Or might they say, "*He* got a B?? My writing is much better than his"? Or "That's not fair. I worked much harder than he did"?

5. What might my colleagues say if I give this student a grade that is much higher than they gave her? (This is especially common in small schools with small departments where teachers often compare students.) Will they think that I am a pushover? that I have no standards?

6. What will the chairperson and the dean say about my overall grades? Will they complain that my grades are out of line with the norm?

7. Do I like this student? If so, has that warped my assessment? If not, has *that* warped my assessment? Have I stored up anger that I can now release? Should I compensate for liking the student by *lowering* my gut assessment of his work? Two related and explosive questions: Do I feel some sexual tension with this student? Do I feel competitive with this student?

8. Does this student act like he or she likes me? hates me? And then two questions that are related to the final ones in number 7: Do I think that this student feels some sexual tension in his or her interactions with me? Do I think that this student is competing with me?

9. Do I agree with this student's politics and values? If the essay I am grading is about an issue that I have a strong opinion about—for example, reproductive rights, gun control, social welfare funding, and so on—has that shaped my evaluation in any way?

10. What grade did I give this student last semester? Is this a make-up (or make-down) call for an earlier assessment that was overly harsh or lenient ? Should it be?

11. How would I feel if I were this student and I got this grade from me? How did I feel when I was a student and received what I took to be an unfair grade?

12. What do I know about this student's personal life that would explain why he did not do as well as he could have (roommate trouble, death in the family, class tensions, etc.)?

13. What do I know about my own personal life that would explain why I identified or did not identify with this student and his or her position or experience in this essay?

Not all of those questions are going on in my head every time I read—at least not consciously. But many of them are there much of the time and I would argue that they play a significant role in the grades that I ultimately give.

I suspect that I am making some readers uncomfortable by acting as if writing instruction is like family counseling or an arbitration hearing, as if there is not a clear right or wrong, a clear better or worse—only a contextualized thick description. But isn't this the case? Isn't grading so difficult because it forces us to ask these questions? And don't we compound the difficulty by chastising ourselves for not being objective or by ignoring the crucial role we play in every grade?

Again I want to argue that while self-recognition does not solve or even simplify problems, it at least gives us the potential to respond differently. Knowledge of our own associations, biases, and beliefs can help us respond more effectively in a conference and through a grade. I've heard Don Murray say many times that a good conference is one the student leaves wanting to keep working on that paper; I would argue that a good conference is one the student leaves wanting to keep working on that paper but *also* that the teacher leaves wanting to keep *reading* it. We need to use the same rule of thumb in developing a grading system; that is, what grading system will keep the students *and* us working at the right level of tension, one that is not so caught up with grades that we spend our time worrying about them but one that does not ignore their powerful influence on student writing and teacher reading?

Grading and Interpersonal Relationships

The question I asked at the beginning of this chapter is, how do we assess student writing—which, for better and mostly worse, is part of our job, responsibility, burden, and power—without destroying the writing relationships we are working so hard to establish in the classroom? Though grades are necessarily and inherently imperfect, some methods seem more consistent with the goals and methods of process teaching; that is, some methods contribute (or at least are less destructive) to healthy and productive teacher-student relationships. For example, a contract grading system, in which the teacher agrees at the beginning of the semester to award a student a particular grade if a student agrees to produce a certain quantity and quality of work, is at least based on a model of reciprocity and negotiation.

I think the same is true of portfolio assessment. Although there are dozens of portfolio systems, almost all ask students to submit a number of different pieces for a final single grade; most ask students to play a role in choosing the work to be evaluated; and some ask students to play a significant role in that evaluation. The idea is to emphasize process, revision, quantity, range—and student involvement. Since the student may have chosen which writing to include and exclude and even may have offered her own assessments of the included pieces, the teacher may see himself less as someone who demands a specific type of essay and more as someone who wants to help the student produce what she sees as her best work.

Of course, critics argue that these are just fancier versions of the same old power relations: whether there is a contract or a portfolio, teachers still give out the grades in the end. And while that criticism is basically true, the fact that we are using a different language for assessment, the fact that we are trying to make our criteria public and even partly negotiable, the fact that we are trying to demystify grading, are in themselves significant.

But while I believe that the assessment system we establish is significant, it is only the general outline against which the real issues of assessment are played out. Whether a teacher uses a points or a contract or a portfolio system, she still must ultimately make judgments and give grades. And at that point it makes less sense to focus on large systems and more sense to focus once again on the particular student-teacher relationships in the classroom. Every time I read, respond to, and grade an essay, I am also reading the student who wrote it; I am reading my own associations into that text; and I am reading the relationship I have and am trying to establish with that student. In other words, while I am reading the text on the page, I am also wondering how hard the student worked on this draft, how capable she is of revision, to what extent my own biases are shaping my responses, and so on.

None of this sounds, or is, consistent with the usual rhetoric of fairness and objectivity that surrounds and dominates assessment research. But it is consistent with a process approach to the teaching of writing. As Tom Romano argues:

> When I evaluate papers, I bring to bear my history as a writer, my tastes in reading, my prejudices and moods, my ever-developing understanding of teenagers, and my perceptions of how a particular student will be affected by what I say. Yes, who the student is helps determine what grade I give, what response I make. It cannot be otherwise. Each of my students is an individual. A paper of similar quality may be a C for Mary, and an A for Max. (114)

Romano's comments are unsettling to those who tell their students that as teachers they are objective, fair, and impartial readers; it is one thing to admit that the same essay would receive a different grade from different teachers but another thing to admit that it would receive different grades from the same teacher if written by different students. But I think Romano points us in the right direction by suggesting that our grades reflect our own attitudes and tastes as much as they reflect something about the essay in front of us.

Still, none of this answers the pragmatic questions. So what should we do about grades? While I am reluctant to say "Here is a grading system that works" or "Here is a system that will create or foster good relationships," I am not reluctant to say "Here are some suggestions that I think will help integrate grading, the establishment of productive classroom relationships, and the teaching of writing:

1. Acknowledge to yourself, your students, and your colleagues that assessment is personal, messy, and contextual.

By openly acknowledging the subjective, interpersonal nature of assessment, we actually become better, more effective writing teachers (and perhaps better teachers in general). We become better because when we assess writing by looking at it within the teacher-student relationship, we are forced to become more involved, more emotionally engaged, more willing (to use Vygotsky's useful model) to live and work in the student's "zone of proximal development." My own experience has been that once I acknowledge all these factors, I am strangely liberated. I still struggle, even agonize, but I now know that it is not because I am an inexperienced, naive, unskilled teacher; rather it is because grading is bound to be stressful and any grade is bound to be arbitrary to some extent. That does not liberate me to give up on the process altogether; instead the knowledge that there isn't a single inherently correct and inherently fair grade for each text and student (a grade I never feel confident that I've discovered) frees me to do my best knowing that in the end, it is all I can do.

I suspect that some teachers worry that by acknowledging the degree to which grades are idiosyncratic or arbitrary or even unfair, we will invite frustration, bitterness, even anarchy, from our students. I've found the opposite is true. Making the messiness of grading public is almost always healthy in a writing class. There is never a danger that grades will lose all meaning, because they are so deeply embedded in our culture and consciousness, but we can make them a little less threatening—to our students and ourselves—by exposing the process.

I find it helpful to talk with students early in the class about goals and expectations and standards. I try as hard as possible to make my grading system clear and consistent. But before I give any grade, I also find it helpful to talk about the way that readers—including teachers—create meaning when they read, about what I take to be the myth of objectivity. I usually ask students whether they expect me to be "objective" and "fair." They always say they do. Then I ask them whether they believe that any reader can possibly be objective about and fair to every single text he encounters. I cite extreme cases—a pro-life student writing for a pro-choice teacher, a soap opera fanatic writing for a teacher who hates TV—and I suggest that a teacher's politics, values, tastes, unconscious motives, will inevitably shape reading and grading.

In fact, I warn my students about the kind of difficulties that I might have with certain sorts of positions they may take (the kind of difficulties that I describe in Chapter 2). I may say something like, "The same essay would certainly receive different grades from different teachers. That may be frustrating but it's inevitable. Fortunately or unfortunately, you're stuck with me this semester." At the same time I also reassure students that I will certainly take the task of grading seriously, that I will try to be aware of my own biases and to struggle against them. By allowing and even encouraging this sort of discussion, a teacher can demystify part of the process and thus neutralize at least some of the unproductive anxiety most student writers experience.

2. Try, whenever possible, to use assessment as a source as well as a measurement of learning.

As long as we're stuck with grades, we need to try to make them a productive part of the teacher-student relationship. It makes sense to offer a positive assessment (through a grade, written report, or verbal comment) to a writer who needs and deserves encouragement and to offer a negative assessment (or at least the conscious withholding of a positive assessment) to a writer who needs and deserves to be provoked. As I argue in the chapter on conferencing (Chapter 3), I believe that students need to find a productive level of tension, and certainly assessment plays a key role in regulating that tension.

The role of assessment is perhaps clearest when we're not doing it. In some ways and at some times, it is harder and more significant not to give grades than to give them (perhaps this is a little like Annie Dillard's point in "To Fashion a Text" that when writing an autobiography it is as important to know what to leave out as it is to know what to include). Stop giving grades and they remain just as significant. In fact, although we like to believe that we can relieve tension by not grading, the opposite is often the case. When we stop giving grades, everyone gets tense—students, parents, administrators, teachers. Well, I'm not sure this tension is bad. If it leads to questioning, to action, to self-assessment, then it serves a productive purpose in the writing course.

3. Develop a system that conflicts as little as possible with your goals and methods.

I use portfolios not because they are inherently better than all other methods but because I want my students to feel a sense of control and responsibility. We all produce some awful stuff, and it helps a writer's attitude to know that not every piece counts, that she has some control over what is *and is not* going to be assessed. I use portfolios also because they suggest that process matters. "Show your work," I'm saying to students, "and you can get credit even if you come up with the 'wrong answer.' " And, finally, I use portfolios because they reflect the range and diversity (or lack of each) of a semester of writing.

As I explain earlier, one reason I don't grade drafts is because I believe that a certain amount of unresolved tension is productive. Another reason I don't is because I want to keep alive the revision process and the notion that essays are dynamic but slow to evolve; I tell students that there are no bad papers, just good papers that haven't arrived yet. I tell them what I learned about early drafts from William Stafford ("Lower Your Standards," *Shoptalk* 76) and from Donald Murray ("Write Dumbly," *Shoptalk* 69). I tell them that places where writing falls apart—in terms of grammar, mechanics, syntax, organization, logic—are the spots that would normally earn students the most points off but are usually the richest parts of the text. I tell them that I can't grade a draft because neither of us knows what it will become in its final form.

Finally, I tell them that correctness counts in their final drafts but not in their rough drafts. I look at mechanics late in the process not because they are not important but because I want students to focus first and foremost on content. But there is another reason. Over the past several years, I have developed a relatively high tolerance for mechanical errors. They just don't bother me as much as they used to. Now I'm not sure this is a virtue, but it does explain why *I* don't make a bigger deal about errors early in the process. My point is not that every teacher should adopt this attitude toward error but rather that all teachers should strive to know their own levels of tolerance and intolerance, likes and dislikes, and factor those into the criteria they use for grading.

4. Separate grading as much as possible from other kinds of responding.

As I say at the beginning of this chapter, I don't think it is possible for teachers or students to forget about grades completely. Still it is possible for teachers to emphasize or deemphasize them more or less directly at certain strategic points in the writing process and writing course. I used to try to make my grade part of the formal response to a student; my written comments therefore tended to be very defensive and pedantic, because I felt I needed to justify the grade on the last page. Over the last several years I've come to realize that responses are usually more effective when separated from assessment. When grading, I am usually evaluating, judging, ranking; when responding, I am often suggesting, free associating, playing. When we read without assessing we are thinking, "What would make this better? What could I suggest?" And, similarly, it is much easier to grade without worrying about responding. In fact, it is relatively easy and pain-free to respond without grading just as it is relatively easy and pain-free to grade without responding. As a result, when I respond to a draft that I am not grading, I find that it goes relatively fast and—gasp!—that I actually enjoy it. Of course, in the end, I am forced to combine these two roles, forced to turn some of my open-ended, suggestive narrative comments into final, absolute letter grades: I don't fool myself about that. But in the meantime I find I am more useful to my students and myself if I keep these tasks separate.

Conclusion

Originally this chapter had no conclusion; it just ended with a final suggestion:

5. Punt.

That the chapter now ends another way is just one more testament to the editor-writer relationship that shapes my own writing and revision processes. When Philippa Stratton first read this chapter, she jotted down two words on the bottom of the last page: "Something missing?" As soon as I saw her comment, I knew she was right. Of course, there was something missing. I meant for "Punt" to be humorous, honest, maybe a little self-deprecating, as if I didn't want my readers to take any of the advice I had just given too seriously after all. But Philippa was right: it was glib, cynical, and I guess not particularly funny. Worse, it was just one more attempt on my part to avoid the messiness and significance of grading.

But what exactly was missing? Like one of Professor Agassiz's students searching to discover the secret characteristics of those damn fish he made them observe for hours and days and weeks, I wondered what exactly the teacher wanted. Maybe she meant that the chapter was incomplete because I offered no clear criteria and guidelines for grading. But I thought I had already suggested that criteria and guidelines reflect individual, perhaps idiosyncratic, values and biases, and that the key is not to adopt someone else's criteria but to become more conscious and self-reflective about our own.

And yet—and perhaps this was the problem Philippa identified—by working only as individual teachers on the grading systems in our classes, we end up capitulating—without so much as a whisper—to the traditional forces that make grading so powerful and positivist in the first place. By accepting what I accepted so easily at the beginning of this chapter about the futility of questioning such an entrenched institution, we end up authorizing and perpetuating that very entrenchment.

Maybe Philippa was chastising me for this cynicism, chastising me for all the times I've thought or said, "Even though grading has ruined my writing class, I can't change what I do because (choose one or more) my department head, principal, dean, students' parents, conscience would never let me" or "I wish I could give all A's, but of course, I can't do *that!*" Maybe she was reminding me of how isolated and vulnerable I felt during those years of teaching at a private high school where every low grade I gave was scrutinized by a headmaster worried about declining enrollment and those years at a Catholic college where every high grade was scrutinized by a registrar who believed that too many A's reflected a lack of standards and an inflation of mediocrity.

How many teachers, I wondered, felt as I have—that my relationships with my students have been adversely defined and shaped by my relationship to the institution in which I work? The more I thought about it, the more I was convinced that I had found the missing link: if traditional systems of assessment are often counterproductive in a writing class, and if we use those systems because they are dictated by the specific and powerful institutions that employ us, then it stands to reason we should not just be tinkering with our grading systems; we should be working to change those institutions.

And so I was ready to end with this final recommendation:

5. Work for institutional policies that will make grading less powerful, damaging, and disruptive.

That is, as teachers, we need to organize, resist, educate; we need to work together to create a better system rather than suffer alone with what we've got; in short, we need to work to change the policies about and attitudes toward grading so that they serve us and our students, not we them.

But though I felt better about this new conclusion, I still couldn't stop worrying about whether Philippa would approve it without requesting revisions. Realizing I was now thinking too little about what I wanted to say or what I thought the text needed and too much about what I thought Philippa wanted to hear, I decided it was time to give her a call. When she answered, I told her, first, that of course I agreed with her, something was missing from the end of the grading chapter, but I wasn't sure exactly what, and I then told her what I had tried and why I thought it made sense, but also why I knew she may have meant a lot of other things but that I wasn't sure I wanted to do all of those things. Finally I shut up and took the direct approach.

"So what did you mean was missing?"

She just laughed. "I didn't have anything specific in mind. For some reason I thought that you may have given me the chapter without the final page or two. That's why I asked, " 'Something missing?' "

So what's the moral of this story? As usual, I'm not certain. Clearly Philippa's open-ended question kept me thinking and writing—which, as I have argued throughout this book, must be a good thing. But good for whom? As a writer of what I thought was a finished text, I craved assessment, approval, praise, closure, a good grade. As a teacher of what I think is an unfinished text, I want to resist symbols or even comments that will create a sense of closure, comfort, finality.

And maybe that is why grading is so inherently charged and messy; it's also why I want to withdraw "punt" and conclude instead with two new open-ended questions:

First, what would happen to our students' writing and to writing relationships if we graded much less and asked "something missing?" much more?

And, second, how will Philippa react if I write her this note on the bottom of this page:

> Please Ms. Stratton, please! Must have approval for this chapter with NO revisions! NO, NO, NO Revisions! Please, Ms. Stratton, Please! NO more revisions!

Hey, it's worth a shot.

Chapter Five

Teaching a Composition Class: Combine and Conquer

It is 8:25 a.m. and I am sitting in a cold, dark classroom watching my students shuffle in. Outside is a sleeting rain and I briefly indulge myself in the fantasy that I am feeling that same "damp, drizzly November in my soul" that Ishmael describes in the opening of *Moby-Dick* (Melville 12)—although *his* feeling drove him to sea in search of the great white whale, while I, decidedly landlocked, sit at a small metal student desk in an antiseptic room that I suddenly realize has none of the things that make a place comfortable—no carpet or couch or green plant or piece of art. By 8:32 I realize something else: eight of the twenty-four students in the class have apparently decided to cut class. The sixteen who have shown up look as miserable as I feel.

"OK, Let's take a look at 'Once More to the Lake,' the E. B. White essay I asked you to read for today," I say in a tone that shows I have been to that lake too many damn times to work up much enthusiasm. Besides, I'm too preoccupied with those eight AWOLers to concentrate fully.

"What do you think he is getting at in this essay?" Not exactly an inspired or inspiring opening question but still I find myself resenting the ensuing silence. "Did anything surprise you about the piece? the ending?" Still no response. No one makes eye contact. Some start thumbing through the text. I suspect, no, I can tell, that they have not read it before. In fact, some students actually start reading it now.

"Did you like it?" A nice open-ended question but, given my already fallen spirit, I am afraid there is some cynicism, even accusation, in my voice. I decide to wait them out.

75

"What happened at the end anyway?" Kim asks. "Did the father die of a heart attack or something?"

"No, he didn't die. Can anyone explain what is going on in that paragraph?" More silence. I wonder: is that another dumb question? Shouldn't I drop the Socratic, guess-what-I'm-thinking and just explain it?

Megan mercifully speaks up: "Isn't he just realizing that one day he will die? I think that's the whole point—that he thinks that he can go back in time but then in the end he realizes that he can't?"

I nod.

Kim again: "But what does that have to do with pulling on a wet swimming suit?"

They all stare some more at the last paragraph. I glance at my watch. Four minutes gone, only forty-six to go. I kill one of those forty-six waiting for someone to answer Kim's question.

Finally, a response and not surprisingly it is Megan again, one of those students who is always trying to bail the class out: "Maybe because a wet swimming suit is cold, like death, in a way? You know what I mean?"

I do but I look around to see if I can get some others involved. Jack has not taken off his hat or coat. His books sit in a pile on his desk. His elbow rests on the top book, his chin rests on his hand. At least he's awake. Julie looks as if she's already dozed off. What's wrong with these kids? When I was a college student, I was prepared for class. At least I think I was. I occasionally answered the teacher's questions and I certainly never fell asleep.

"Maybe we need a sense of the whole essay before we can figure out the end. What do you think is the relationship between White— the narrator—and his father? I mean, how is that relationship related to the one between White and his son?"

The students stare at the text, waiting for inspiration—or maybe for someone else to try an answer. I stare right at Mike, who hasn't even opened his book, daring him, willing him, to speak up, and miraculously, he does: "Could you repeat the question?"

I do, this time making it a little more coherent. A few students hazard half-hearted answers and I make an equally half-hearted attempt to pull the students through an analysis of E. B. White's views of death and immortality, of recurring symbols and images, of mixed diction and the repetition of certain grammatical structures. But as I ramble on, I am becoming increasingly distracted and irritated. I find myself thinking about how much better my 10:30 class is than this one, my 8:30; about what a great discussion we had last semester when I taught "Once More to the Lake"; about how great it would be to teach somewhere else, somewhere where the students not only read the assigned texts but come in with engaged expressions and thoughtful questions and perceptive observations.

I glance at my watch—still twenty minutes to get through—and so I do what I usually do when the class is struggling:

"Please take out a sheet of paper. I'd like you to write something now." I should have started with writing; I usually do, but I sensed that none of us today were up to something quite so strenuous as taking out a sheet of paper. And, in fact, the students open their journals with about as much enthusiasm as they showed toward the White piece. Maybe I should surprise them. I imagine myself saying, "How about a little pop quiz?" in the sort of voice that the witch used when she asked the scarecrow about fire. I also imagine with some guilty pleasure the power I would feel if they displayed surprised and desperate expressions. But instead I follow my usual route:

"I'd like you do some freewriting for a few minutes. White is remembering a lake that he went to as a child and he's remembering how everything looked and sounded and smelled. I want you to write about your memories of a place that you went to with your family as a child."

While we are writing, I calm down a bit. I think about how little I've done to inspire passion or excitement about the White essay, about how dull and uninspired my questions have been, about how I usually start out trying to relate what they've read to their personal experiences. I think about the things in my own life that are distracting me this morning: the promise that I made and broke to myself to have spent the weekend working on a revision of an article that's already a month overdue; the fact that Emma complained of a stomachache right before she trudged out to the bus stop; the weird squeak my car made every time I turned right; and so on.

So rather than write about my own memories of lake vacations, I start writing about how to get the class on my side or maybe me on theirs. Of course, it's relatively easy to identify what's wrong; it's much tougher to figure out a solution. The things I usually do (or at least am tempted to do) when a class is bombing are not particularly productive: sometimes, like when the "boyz 'n the hats" were giving me a hard time, I try intimidation: "Go ahead," I say as I reach in my holster for my grade book, "make my day." Other times I try preaching: "I know you don't think there is much to this whole writing thing. You think it's not worth your time, maybe you think it's a hoax. Well, let me tell you: I used to be like you once. I too was lost and alone. But then I discovered the joy of writing. And now . . ." More often I try to induce guilt: "When I think about all the freedom I've given you, all the chances, and this is how you treat me . . . well, I could almost die!"

In perhaps my worst moments I try to divide and conquer, to complain to the "good" students about the "bad" ones. It is, of course, a pathetic strategy: "I know that some of you are working really hard and I'm really pleased with your work. Unfortunately, though, for a class of this sort to work, everyone needs to make an effort and there are people in here who are not contributing anything." I wonder where I learned to teach like that? Was it from Mrs. Pollack, my fourth-grade teacher, who used to lecture us in exasperation and disapproval: "I am sorry that some of you have to sit and have your precious time wasted by your classmates who are apparently just too immature to listen to what I am trying to teach." And then perhaps worst of all: "Why can't the rest of you be more like Jeremy and Diane?" thereby guaranteeing not only that we would hate Mrs. Pollack but that we would also hate poor Jeremy Mandell and Diane Rosen.

Or maybe I learned it from Pogo, the clown my parents hired to entertain at my fifth birthday party. According to family legend, as soon as he started to perform, I burst into tears, yelling, "I'm scared; I want him to leave." Pogo was upset, then embarrassed and hurt, and finally very angry. And so as he left the party he went over to the other kids and asked: "You liked the show, didn't you? And you wanted to see more of it. But now you can't and it's all because of Laddy. Don't you think Laddy is a little crybaby?"

The five minutes I planned to give my students is already long past. "OK, would one of you like to read what you've written?" No one looks at me. This time I try humor. "Look, let's try to talk one at a time so everyone can be heard." A few weak smiles, but still no luck. I push on anyway. "Come on, is this a comp class or an oil painting?" resorting to the Henny Youngman school of one-liners. "Look, it's an awful day; we all wish we had stayed in bed like your classmates who couldn't be here with us today, but we didn't so we might as well make the best of it." A few of them smile. They are not cheering and carrying me on their shoulders (after all, this isn't *Dead Poets Society* stuff), but at least we're not as far on our different sides.

"So what did you come up with? Would anyone like to read what you've got?" To my relief and great gratitude, several hands go up.

Jenny reads a hilarious paragraph about fighting with her brother in the backseat of their family's Buick on the annual car trip. "One year I actually put a line of masking tape down the middle of the seat and if he even *looked* on my side of the tape I would yell, "Mom! Dad! John is bothering me!" Mike reads a page about his annual visits to his grandparents in Canada, and his thinking for some inexplicable reason that everything—the lake, his grandparents' house, his grandparents—was shrinking year by year. Finally, Maura reads her freewriting; it's about her family's reunion when she was nine. She remembers spending her time watching her father and brothers and uncles play softball and her mother and aunts and grandmother "cook and gossip and clean up" and feeling the whole time that she did not fit into either group.

Now I am excited and I launch into a brief minilecture: "In your own pieces, in the personal narrative essays that you are working on for your next conference, you might want to choose that sort of observation—like Maura's watching the men and women and feeling left out of both groups: that's a great moment—and then play with it, try to relate it to something else. Ask yourself questions about the thing you've noticed: what caused it to happen? What effect did it have? How is it like or unlike other experiences and memories you associate with it? The memory or moment doesn't have to be a major event. It can be a small thing—like Mike's seeing how small his grandparents' house looks or like Jenny's remembering about the tape on the backseat—and then you can discover its hidden meaning. Remember when Dillard wrote about turning sight into insight? That's what I'm asking you to try to do."

A few people look as if that made sense, but I know that for others it will be meaningless until I am discussing their own essays with them. Was I right to take over the discussion? Just as in a one-to-one conference, it is difficult to know when to take over a class and tell them what I think and believe and when to lead them to take over, to talk to each other. And so I turn back to the class: "Any other responses?"

Kevin responds. "I know what Mike means because when I went back to my old elementary school, I couldn't believe how tiny the desks and stuff were. But about your grandparents? I mean, who knows? Old people *do* shrink."

As the students respond to each other's descriptions and memories, I try to think of a graceful transition to bring us back to E. B. White and to possible connections between "Once More to the Lake" and the personal narrative pieces they are working on. But it's 9:17 and I know that the transition will make more sense once they've all read White's piece.

"OK, look. I wanted to talk more about White, but we're running out of time and I know half of you haven't read any of it . . . or all of you have read half of it or something like that. Which is too bad because he's writing about a lot of the same stuff that you're all writing about in your pieces. So for Friday you have to read the White essay . . . or come in wearing a wet swimming suit."

This seems to get Kevin's attention. "Read it or wear a wet swimming suit? How long is the essay anyway?" The class laughs, finally.

Root Metaphors for Teaching

Was that a good class? I'm not sure. Do students learn to write by hearing me talk about writing? I'm not even sure about that anymore. When I first started this job, I taught writing in an extremely directive way. I often assigned topics and I usually assigned the form (I was particularly partial to the five-paragraph essay). I spent class time talking mostly about deductive and inductive reasoning, thesis statements, and transitions. I remember doing minilessons on subordination and parallel construction. Whenever I talked about writing, I spent a lot of time on my feet in front of the class; I was usually at the board or the opaque projector.

I didn't think much about the kinds of writing relationships I was creating in the classroom. Ironically, though, when I taught literature, I rarely lectured and we usually sat in a circle. During our literary discussions I tried to create an atmosphere that was informal yet serious, lively yet focused. I often asked students about their personal experiences and I tried to get them to relate those experiences to the texts we were reading.

Why such a difference? I can no longer remember what I was thinking at the time but I suspect that I was just following the examples I had been shown when I was a student. None of my own teachers—in high school or college—taught writing as an ongoing process of discovery or revision; in fact, I thought I was being pretty open-minded by moving even a little away from the "three/three five-paragraph essays" that I wrote as a high schooler (in each of our five-paragraph essays we needed to have three subpoints to support our thesis and three specific examples to support each subpoint). On the other hand, many of these same teachers used innovative, reader-response approaches when we turned to literature.

So it wasn't as if I was unaware of alternate pedagogical approaches; it's just that I hadn't yet figured out that those approaches could be applied to the teaching of writing. Once I did—that is, once I read Murray and Macrorie, Emig and Elbow; once I placed student writing at the center of the course; once I began to emphasize individual voice, discovery, and revision; once I began to respond to writing in one-to-one conferences; once I began to allow group work and collaborative composing; once I did all that—everything changed.

Well, almost everything—because, in spite of all the freedom I now give my classes, in spite of all the conferences and small-group work, there still are moments and days when I still need and want to be in charge, to be extremely directive. The problem, then, is not only how to change the focus and organization of the course but also how to change with it. In other words, what role am I supposed to play in this new type of classroom? Clearly my new role is less directive, but I still want and need to give some directions; clearly I want to be less of an authoritarian about the writing process, but I still want and need to be an authority.

As I point out in the introduction to this teacher-student section, I certainly understand those writing teachers who want to reject their power and status in the classroom ("I just want to be a facilitator" or "I just want to be another member of this community of writers"). But as I argue earlier, as much as I like the democratic, egalitarian rhetoric of that model, it is simply not plausible or, for that matter, desirable. We have power in this situation, and though we may not like to admit it, part of the thrill of teaching and of being taught has to do with the way we use that power. We may decide to allocate some of it, share it with our colleagues and our students, but the fact remains that it was ours in the first place.

Still, even with this power, a reassuringly small number of us are the dominant, powerful figure we used to be when we played school by standing at a chalkboard and pointing a stick at the other children. So who are we now when we teach in front of a class? In order to understand our role when we are relating to a group of students, it is useful to think less literally and more metaphorically. In other words, when we teach we are . . . what else? . . . teachers, but what does that mean? What model do we use? What metaphors do we teach from? Donald Murray, for example, likes to talk about the teacher as a craftsperson, the students as apprentices (*A Writer*). But that fits better with the one-to-one approach, where we sit side by side, watching, modeling, suggesting. In the classroom the dynamic is very different.

Our relationship with the whole class is not just the sum of the individual relationships we have established. I have learned the hard way that the same student may be deferential and polite and even vulnerable in a one-to-one conference and become aggressively rebellious in the large group (*The Lord of the Flies* syndrome). Or a student who seems painfully shy and reserved in class may be witty, gregarious, silly, and outspoken in her conferences. Part of my job, then, is to try to bridge this gap, to help students "be themselves" in front of one another; but another part of my job is to learn to accept this gap and to respond to it.

Our vision of ourselves as writing teachers is and needs to be different when we are relating to one student from when we are relating to the whole group. And I would argue that students see their relationship to us when they are dealing with us privately in a conference as different from when they are dealing with us publicly in a classroom (consider, for example, the conciliatory posture Jack adopted in my office versus the more provocative pose he assumed in front of his peers). I am convinced that students see us as a different kind of figure (perhaps even a different figure altogether) when we stand up in front of the class than when we sit beside them in an office conference.

In a one-to-one conference, we must seem like a counselor or a psychotherapist or doctor of some type, perhaps a midwife. But when we speak to twenty-five students at once about what we expect from them and why we expect it, who do they see us as then? Talk show hosts doing a monologue? Drill sergeants terrorizing new recruits? Evangelists addressing the congregation? Perhaps more to the point, who do we seem to be to ourselves? Are we doctors talking to patients? Parents speaking to our children? Encounter group leaders talking to participants? These root metaphors for teaching are significant because they not only reflect but also shape what we do in the classroom. Of course, none of us play the same role each time we teach, but I am convinced that we each have certain root metaphors that inform our behavior. And I am also convinced that each of the metaphors suggests a different kind of relationship with our students.

The key question for me is this: how does my relationship to the class as a whole contribute to—or interfere with—my effort to establish a productive relationship with each student? It is clear by now that I often think of one-to-one writing instruction in terms of psychotherapy, but I find myself playing very different roles and trying to establish very different relationships when I interact with the class as a whole. In fact, by prompting myself to freewrite about what roles I play when I teach, I realized that there are four dominant metaphors that shape my own interactions and relationships with the class:

The Teacher as Performer, The Class as Audience

There are definitely times when I feel as if I am on stage. In fact, I sometimes have a flash of myself in Vegas ("I want to change the mood now. Can we bring the house lights down a bit?"). I realize that this metaphor—the teacher as actor or performer—runs counter to many teachers' self-image. It is too artificial, too dramatic, too unilateral. But it seems to me that at least to some extent this role is inevitable—and healthy. Students pay money to be taught. We get paid money to teach. We can talk a lot about peer teaching, decentering authority, collaboration, but many students, like Chauncey Gardener in Kozinski's novel *Being There* ("I just like to watch"), expect to be entertained. And, perhaps more to the point, many of us chose to become teachers because we wanted the chance to be on stage. I'm not suggesting that this is our only or even our primary role; I am saying that it is one important and potentially positive aspect of the teacher-class relationship.

And if we are often performers, then our class is our audience. That explains in part why I am so bothered when students read or gossip or fall asleep or play hookey while I am performing. It also explains why students often feel frustrated: watching performances is sometimes satisfying but it is a relatively passive role. Just as different cultures establish different narratives—determining who is allowed to tell stories—different classrooms determine different entertainment and digression rights. Who, for example, is allowed to say, "A funny thing happened to me on the way to class"? In most classrooms, only the teacher.

I'm not suggesting that I think of teaching as a series of skits or acts; there are moments (and I'll describe some below) when this metaphor seems inadequate or inappropriate. But there are other moments when performance, particularly humor, seems necessary and productive. Sometimes we need to use humor to defuse tension between our students and ourselves, or between one student and another. Other times we need to use humor in a self-deprecating way to acknowledge out loud what everyone in the room already knows: this class today is bombing. I don't think this is something that can be scripted or carefully planned ("Three prepositional phrases walk into a bar . . ."), but it also should not be underestimated. Some students are occasionally going to see us as performers (when you ask students what makes a good teacher, an overwhelming number mention sense of humor) whether we see ourselves that way or not; the question is what sort of performance we give them.

Teacher as Dinner Party Host, Students as Guests

I know that "party" suggests a frivolous, indulgent, unintellectual activity (particularly now that it is used as a verb), but I have in mind a different sort of party. Like characters in a Trollope or Woolf novel, teachers spend a lot of time planning and throwing thoughtful parties. In our case, the guests are our students and, like all guests, they need to be looked after. We need to provide some sort of nourishment, and entertainment needs to be planned. We need to make sure everyone is comfortable (or perhaps—to keep things lively—just comfortable enough). As a host of a party or of a class, I often like there to be a certain edge, an air of expectation and anticipation.

How do we do this? Most of us not only make an effort to get to know our writing students; we also make an effort to help them get to know one another. We may have them interview each other and then write it up; we may pair up two "guests" who we know have something—hometown, hobby, politics, writing style—in common; we may make comments in class that are designed to connect students ("So, Robert, would you agree with what Diane said yesterday about . . .").

Our goal is to keep things lively and to keep everyone actively involved—even if they are involved primarily through listening. We participate in the activities of the party with the guests; but as the hosts, we are the ones ultimately responsible for preparation and for crisis control. And while this is another metaphor that suggests our greater responsibility and control, it is a very different one from the performer metaphor. Perhaps more female than male, perhaps more nurturing and less self-aggrandizing. In this model, our job is not to tell students what they should think and know and feel, but rather to bring them together, to take care of their needs so that they can flourish and enjoy themselves, to listen to them, to let them take the floor when they are comfortable doing so.

Teacher as Parent, Student as Adolescent Children

I have already confessed to moments of exasperation in which I deliver what I hope will be a guilt-inducing speech in a sorrowful and moralistic tone. It is a tone that—to me, anyway—seems parental. Oddly enough I have almost never used this tone when talking to a student in a conference, but somehow it seems useful or at least irresistible when I am dealing with the whole class. And so a few times per semester I suddenly find myself in the middle of a finger-wagging, head-shaking warning about how "Some of you seem to think that you can blow this class off, show up whenever you feel like it, work whenever you feel like it . . . well, I have news for you . . ." Of course, this lecture is usually delivered on a day like the one I just described—when the students who most need to hear it have ditched class.

Although I recognize the riskiness of this approach and its utter lack of dignity, I am not certain that it is altogether unproductive for the class as a whole. On my side of the relationship, it indicates a care and concern that some students appreciate (though I can tell that others simply pity me for taking the whole thing so seriously); on their side it at the very least gives them a common enemy, someone to push against, someone they can band together to defy or at least gossip about.

But that is only part, perhaps the least noble part, of the parent-child relationship in the classroom. There are other times when I see them—and this will sound too much like Jerry Lewis—as "my kids."

I feel that way when I am proud of them for the way they relate to each other, for what they have accomplished as a group. And there are still other times when I want to protect them, times when I identify them with my own daughters or with myself when I was eighteen years old. Whenever that happens, whenever I look around the room and see them as somebody's children, whenever I allow myself to remember the excitement, complexity, confusion, chaos, and pain of young adulthood, then I find myself more empathic, more ready to try to understand their deficiencies, more willing to try to see things from their perspectives—even when I'm confronted with those provocative blank stares and yawns and eye-rolls and watch-glances.

Once again, I fear that many teachers and many students will find this metaphor—teaching as parenting—to be presumptuous and inappropriate. I understand why talking about teaching as parenting is unpopular and uncool: it emphasizes the unequal power relationship we don't like to acknowledge, much less discuss; it makes the teaching of writing sound unscholarly and unprofessional (one "professional" compositionalist complained to me recently: "You're talking about teaching as psychotherapy? as parenting? God, those are exactly the kinds of popular images of comp we've been trying so hard to get away from these last ten years"); and it makes us examine our own unconscious fantasies, motives, and associations toward our student.

In spite of (and partly because of) all that, I think we need to explore this metaphor. The reality is that we are not their parents and our mission in the classroom is for the most part very different from parenting. But just as I argued that there is important and useful overlap between teaching and psychotherapy, I believe that it is instructive to think about how many of the same issues, tensions, and pleasures are raised by parenting and the teaching of writing.

Teacher as Preacher, Students as Congregation

There are definitely moments when I feel like a preacher (or, in my case, a rabbi) addressing a congregation. They are those moments when I am trying to be wise and reflective and inspirational, moments when I am trying to tell them about the wonderful and powerful and mysterious nature of writing, moments when I am talking about voice and self and honesty. I know the dangers of this metaphor: Hashimoto and other critics have pointed out disdainfully that this kind of talk has an "evangelical," anti-intellectual character ("Voice"). But while I am just as disdainful of evangelicalism as the next academician, I find it occasionally useful and irresistible to talk about writing in terms usually reserved for transcendent experiences.

Don't get me wrong: I've never suggested that writing, even those beloved personal narratives of self-actualizing events, can make a blind man see; I always resist calling the one-to-one conference "confession"; and I try to avoid referring to myself as a holy man too many times in a class hour. But the fact is we are given the opportunity, perhaps even the mission, to be charismatic figures in the writing classroom. And we are given the mission to bring writing to the masses.

These are not the only models or metaphors I teach by: sometimes I feel like a sensitivity group leader, other times like a political candidate, occasionally like a wallflower at a party I stumbled into by mistake. My point is not that there is one correct or preferable metaphor for teaching. (I am aware that my own background, my gender, my politics, my personal relationships, make my own metaphors distinctive, if not downright idiosyncratic.) Instead I am suggesting, once again, that we all need to become more reflective about our own choices and to consider the positive and negative implications of those choices.

And I am suggesting two other things: first, we need to consider how our relationship to the whole class—whatever that relationship may be—supports or interferes with the one-to-one relationships we are trying to establish through our responses to each student's writing. As I have tried to point out, though I play a different role in the conference and in class, I try to make these roles complementary. Sometimes that isn't easy. For example, in a conference, I want to make a student realize how much I care about him and his writing, so I concentrate as fully and as personally as possible on everything he says; however, in class, because I want the group to feel as if I am interested in them equally, I often try not to follow up too much on the comments of any one student.

Second, we need to consider how our own associations and behaviors intersect with the associations and behaviors of our students. In other words, it is important to remember that how we see the teacher-class relationship may be very different from the way the students see it (see Tobin "Bridging Gaps"). In fact, whenever I have asked my students to talk about *their* role, to respond metaphorically to a prompt about writing in high school and college courses ("Writing is like . . ."), many use metaphors that reflect their feelings of frustration with, powerlessness over, and detachment from not only the writing process but also the teacher-student relationship. Many students compare writing to going to the dentist, to taking a test for a driver's license, to trying to get out of bed on a school day. Again and again, student writers describe writing as doing something they hate—getting a medical checkup, doing household chores, doing homework—because they know it is good for them.

And so the role we play in class as an authority figure of some kind may create two related problems: first, it may conflict with the role we play in our individual relationships with each student, and second, it may trigger certain forms of resistance from our students. Still, perhaps these problems are not as serious as they first may seem. It is inevitable that we will play somewhat different roles with different students and even with the same students at different times—as I think most students know already. While it's true, of course, that students don't need a teacher who seems schizophrenic, completely quirky, and unpredictable, they can benefit from realizing that most teachers, like most other people, adopt different personas in different situations.

As for the other problem, we just need to remember that our vision of ourselves as authority figures will often be more noble and more self-serving than our students' view of us. When we are in front of a class (or just in the loudest place in the circle), we may talk about finding a voice, giving birth to an idea, summoning a muse, planting and nurturing and harvesting, traveling to a new and exciting place—which, given our roles as established writers, consciousness raisers, and coaches, makes a lot of sense. But we need to remind ourselves meanwhile that we are often speaking to a group of students who are in class against their interest and will, who are bored, aggravated, and, in some cases, angered by the role we are performing: in other words, while I'm imagining myself a media star or guru, many in the class may see me as a policeman or a dentist.

That still leaves me choices: I can work harder to make it clear to them and to myself who I am trying to be when I teach a class. And then I can make an effort to bridge the gap between how some of them see me and how I see myself. Or I can grit my teeth and hope, for all our sakes, that there's enough novocaine to go around.

Part Two

The Student-Student Relationship

One of the major advances of the process movement has been the tremendous attention paid to creating new relationships between students. Many of the landmark texts of the early movement— Elbow's *Writing Without Teachers*, Macrorie's *Writing to Be Read*, Murray's *A Writer Teaches Writing*—focus on teaching students to teach themselves and each other. The eighties may have began as the "process" decade, but it ended with an emphasis on "collaboration" and "social construction." The rhetoric most of us who teach composition use to describe our own classrooms—we talk about creating "colearners" and a "community of writers"—suggests that students ought to see their interests and goals as shared and cooperative. In the last several years this approach has received theoretical and political justification with the publication of books such as Bruffee's *A Short Course in Writing*, Gere's *Writing Groups*, and LeFevre's *Invention as a Social Act*.

This new emphasis on creating supportive relationships between writing students has no doubt been positive. But just as the teacher as facilitator may be a simplistic overreaction to the authoritarian traditional teacher, the student as colearner or community member also misses the point. While it may be politically correct to promote collaboration, consensus, and public discourse, the truth is that many peer relationships are shaped equally by competition, dissensus, and private interests. The contemporary student-student relationship in the writing class is so often unproductive, I suspect, because it is so often awkwardly defined. In most situations students are neither openly and vigorously competing nor openly and vigorously collaborating; instead they are working together in loosely formed small groups to produce individual and sometimes competing texts. As a result, the roles that students are asked to play are blurred and confusing.

Part of the problem is that we have romanticized and reified the notion of a decentered, supportive, collaborative writing group without paying enough attention to what sorts of peer relationships inhibit writing and what sorts foster it. For example, throughout the research on collaboration, there has been almost no discussion of the role of competition in the writing class or the writing process. Because our students' competitive urges do not fit our self-image and because those urges make us uncomfortable, we tend to ignore or deny that they exist. When competition is acknowledged as a factor in the teaching of writing, it is almost always seen as negative, because it creates a classroom atmosphere that is "stressful, crippling, and counterproductive" (Romano 173).

My own sense, though, is that competition and cooperation are not mutually exclusive or even necessarily conflictual; people often compete in cooperative situations and cooperate in competitive ones. While it is true that intensely competitive assignments can lead to frustration, even resignation, it is also true that writing students—like writing teachers—sometimes produce their best work as a result of their competitive feelings. Before we can analyze and evaluate the role of competition in writing classes, however, we need more information about where, when, and how it manifests itself in interactions between writing students; how we as teachers create and/or neutralize these competitive interactions; and what role competition actually plays in a student's composing process.

Steve's case raises complicated questions here. The support of his peers clearly helped him gain the confidence to try such a risky essay. However, part of his acknowledged motivation was his desire to write an essay "that was as good or better than Brendan's" and the group support for the anti-Semitic portrait shows that the majority may not always be right.

I am not suggesting that we ought to abandon collaborative work or that we return to an authoritarian model. My suggestion is that we be more honest about what is actually going on in our classrooms and that we be less afraid of more intense student-student relationships at either end of the spectrum. In other words, I think we should promote open and productive competition (telling students that we will publish the best essays from the class, for example) and real and full collaboration (occasionally asking students to write something—start to finish—together in small groups, not just use the groups for peer review or brainstorming).

But acknowledging that a productive writing community needs both competition and collaboration still begs the question of how we can help create that productive community in the first place. Some classroom teachers simply announce to their students, "In this course you will become a community of writers," but then do little more to make that happen than tell their students to sit in a circle, encourage them to learn one another's first names, or ask them to respond to one another's essays in small groups. On the other hand, most researchers—I would include here Bartholomae and Petrosky, Patricia Bizzell, and Mike Rose (*Lives*) among many others—immediately jump to a larger issue: how to help students enter the community (or communities) of academic discourse. I am not denying the importance of this issue—I think it is crucial that students eventually come to see themselves as part of that larger community—but, first, we need to pay more attention to how the relationships that students establish with their classmates determine their progress (or lack of progress) as writers.

In this section I look at peer relationships in the writing class by focusing on three specific features of student-student interaction: competition as it manifests itself in the way a writing student responds to her peers and their texts (Chapter 6); identification and modeling as the means by which students learn to see one another and then themselves as writers (Chapter 7); and collaboration in terms of how we structure classroom assignments and interactions (Chapter 8).

Chapter Six

Competition: Beyond the Rhetoric of Collaboration

As I began reading Maura's essay, I thought it was just another "how I won the big high school game" narrative:

> As I walked onto the field, I kept thinking about last week's game. The game against Ewing High. They are a pretty rough team to beat and we had beaten them again. But the team we were playing this time, Hunderton High, is an even larger school and their field hockey team was even better. I looked over at the girls from their team. They were very big and tough looking. The kind of girls you stayed away from. Then I looked at our team. In our whole starting line-up there were only about three girls over the height of 5′ 2″ and over the weight of 110. Sure, this was going to be a fun game.

If you teach Freshman Comp, you're familiar with the genre. Unlike the "how I wrecked the family car" essay, in which the narrator's cockiness leads to disaster, the pattern in the sports essay is reversed: through amazing courage and determination a humble narrator triumphs over overwhelming, Rocky-like odds. But there was something different this time. It wasn't that it was written by a female—the day is long gone when all of the jocks were boys—but that her main rival is one of her own teammates:

> As I walked onto that field this time, I wasn't thinking about our opponents. I was thinking about how I had been benched in that last game. Alright I'll admit it: I had deserved it but being benched for a freshman! Needless to say this was humiliating for a senior, but when the freshman scored, that was the end to a "perfect day." I couldn't let that happen again. NO WAY. I had worked hard at my game for four years, I had won the respect of the coach, and I wasn't

going to let an underclassman ruin it, especially not a freshman that
I taught to play earlier in the season.

By now it is clear that Maura is telling two different stories here: one
is about her team's attempt to defeat their heavily favored opponents
and the other is about her own battle to outplay her freshman teammate. Throughout the essay Maura and the reader struggle to keep
these two themes separate. The turning point comes early in the
second half of the game (and of the essay):

> The next penalty corner I rushed the goalie and Nancy hit the shot.
> I saw a white blur from the corner of my eye and tried to get my
> stick on it, but it was going too fast and the goalie was able to block
> it with her enormous pads before I could get it. But I was somehow
> able to get the rebound and deflect it in. Yes! I had scored and put
> us ahead. Rub that in your face, freshman!

Although Maura is overjoyed that her goal put her team ahead, it is
her struggle with her teammate that dominates her thoughts and that
pushes her to score two more goals:

> The game had turned out great. I did not even mind that the
> freshman was put in the game at the end, because thank God, she
> wasn't subbing for me this time. So I decided that I would satisfy
> my ego even more and help the little freshman out. By the end of
> the game we were ahead 5-1 and I was telling her what to do and
> what not to do, as if I had some kind of authority over her. When
> the final whistle blew I was ecstatic. I never felt so alive in my life!
> Everyone was congratulating me. After talking to a reporter, Coach
> Edmunds called me over, put her arm around me approvingly and
> said, "I know why you played so well; it was because you did not
> want to be showed up by the freshman again, wasn't it? Wasn't it?"
> I just walked away feeling as if I was up in the sky. I had evened the
> score with the freshman and myself. Now I could go back to playing
> the normal field hockey that I had always played.

What struck me about the essay was how much more focused, intense,
and competitive Maura seemed as a field hockey player than she did
as a writer. Of course, field sports and writing are different sorts of
processes, but I kept thinking that there was something for me to learn
here—about how much it meant for her to do well and to outplay the
freshman, about how her competitive feelings had driven her to
terrific accomplishments. I thought about how the coach was keenly
aware of Maura's desire to outplay her teammate, about how she may
even have used that to motivate her, about how she could not relax
and just play the game until she had somehow resolved her fierce
competitive feelings about the freshman, and about how she never felt
so alive in her life as when she succeeded.

Mostly, though, I wondered what part of Maura's experience as an athlete could be transferred to her experience as a writer. Although I had not thought about it much before, I realized that my students often write about intense competitive urges and situations—sometimes, like Maura, about competitive successes but often about failures, such as wrecking the family car while acting on a dare from a friend or rival. The writers of these essays care intensely about their performance and how that performance is being evaluated by authority figures and by their peers. Suddenly I had all sorts of questions. Did they care in the same way about their essays and how others saw them? When students compete as writers, do they choose a particular rival (as Maura had done)? Are their competitive feelings directly related to the way that I treat them? Do males and females respond in identifiably different ways to competition?

Why There Is So Little Literature to Review

When I first tried to answer these questions, I realized how little we talk about these issues—in journals articles, conference presentations, or even faculty lounges. My guess is that most composition teachers have decided long ago that competition is antithetical to the writing process and to the teaching of writing. At some point, we designated competition a "Devil term" and collaboration a "God term," without worrying about the fact that people sometimes collaborate to do terrible things or compete to do good. On what basis have we decided that collaboration and competition are mutually exclusive terms or that competition is necessarily bad for composition?

What may be most striking about the research on competition in writing classes is how little of it exists. I have not come across a single referenced study specifically on competition and composition. Because there is extensive research on related issues such as writing apprehension, assessment, collaborative writing, even student "underlife" in the writing classroom, this failure to examine competitive interaction seems particularly odd. And because so many decisions about pedagogy (such as the use of peer review or group brainstorming) are based on the unproven assumption that students in "noncompetitive" classrooms are more productive than students in "competitive" ones, the need for research in this area seems compelling.

In the few instances in which competition is directly discussed by process writing teachers, it is always treated as a negative force, as a factor to be reduced or eliminated. For example, in *Writing*

Without Teachers, Peter Elbow identifies "competitive," along with words like "rigid," "stubborn," and "aggressive," as part of the "doubting game," the process by which we look for errors or faults in someone else's writing. Although Elbow acknowledges that there is some value in this sort of competitive classroom interaction, he argues that we need more often to play the "believing game." That is, we need to teach writing in ways that are more "cooperative," "flexible," and "nonaggressive."

Similarly, in Clearing the Way, although Tom Romano acknowledges the creative energy that can result when students read and respond in writing to one another's work, he adds: "But I must issue a caution: If the sharing and the pacing among students devolve into vicious competition, then the creative atmosphere can turn stressful, crippling, and counterproductive. The pressure on students to compete with and beat each other will inhibit creativity, will make risking anything too dangerous" (173). Perhaps most interestingly, Romano suggests without explanation that there is something unique about composition that precludes the value of competition: "In many content-area disciplines, of course, competition is the norm. And some students are naturally competitive in any situation. I discourage competition as much as possible, try to value the vision and developing language skill of all of my students" (174).

Perhaps the strongest indictment of competition by a process writing teacher is the research of Anna Shannon Elfenbein. In "Competition: The Worm in the Bud in a Collaborative Seminar," Elfenbein describes a graduate seminar she taught in which several of her students vehemently resisted her efforts to get them to help one another with their writing assignments. Based on her observations of this class, Elfenbein argues that competition leads to "monstrous results," that competition has the "terrible power to cannibalize efforts to promote collaborative learning," and that students who cling to individual "ownership" of essays or ideas destroy the atmosphere of a writing class.

There is merit to warnings and criticisms about the potentially destructive power of competition in a writing class. We have all watched (or worse, participated in) competitive classroom incidents in which students were pitted directly against one another in destructive and unnecessary ways, in which students were pigeonholed as eagles, bluebirds, and, well, pigeons. The point is that none of us who make our living as academics need to be reminded of the tremendous potential for embarrassment, pain, and loss of self-esteem that attends every competitive interaction.

The real question then is not whether there are potentially negative aspects in competitive situations (of course there are), but rather why competition resonates so negatively for so many of us that we have refused even to acknowledge it, much less to examine it, in our classrooms or in ourselves. My own theory is that competition just does not fit neatly or comfortably into the image we have written for ourselves as process writing teachers. We want to believe that our classrooms are a humane and nurturing alternative to the rest of the university and the rest of American culture; rather than reproduce the competitive model in the larger culture, we resist it. All of this makes it particularly difficult to acknowledge that even in our classrooms, even in a context in which collaboration and support and nurturing are advocated and practiced, we and our students are still sometimes motivated by competitive urges.

Because competition is threatening to most of us—politically and psychologically—we have established simple and, I think, naive binary oppositions between social construction and individual voice, collaboration and competition. As a result, most theorists who favor collaboration in writing courses ignore competition altogether, instead focusing their criticism on the notion of individual invention and voice. In the research of Kenneth Bruffee, Karen Burke Lefevre, and James Berlin, for example, the model of social construction of knowledge is presented as a clear political, philosophical, and mutually exclusive alternative to the invention of truth by an individual writer. Patricia Bizzell summarizes this split by arguing that all composition research is either "inner-directed" or "outer-directed" (215). Like Bruffee, Lefevre, and Berlin, she argues that we must begin to pay more attention to how social relations shape our students' writing and how knowledge is socially constructed in the composition classroom.

But for this to happen, we need to see competition as one of those social relations and to understand the role it plays in our classrooms. Unfortunately when competition is mentioned at all, it is usually used not to examine our teaching and students but rather to describe what goes on in the socially and politically incorrect classrooms of other disciplines. For example, Susan Miller worries that although she values "student participation in shared creations and validations of knowledge" (Anderson et al. "Cross-Curricular Underlife" 28), there are teachers across the curriculum "who do not imagine their courses as settings where students compete against themselves in relation to negotiated standards of achievement" (29). The assumption is that students might find our classrooms to be collaborative and noncompetitive but in their other courses they will be forced to face a more individualistic and competitive curriculum. But is there any real evidence that our students feel noncompetitive in our classrooms or even that writers perform better in noncompetitive environments?

The Nature of Competition in One Process Classroom

In order to take a step toward understanding the nature of competition in composition, we need to begin by examining our students and ourselves. The problem is that competitive actions and feelings are difficult to measure or even identify. A student who says that she feels a need or desire to write a better essay than her classmates' essays is obviously acting competitively, but it is often difficult to establish boundaries that clearly distinguish competitive from noncompetitive urges and behavior. The very same action—say, spending many hours revising an essay—could be competitive or noncompetitive depending on the particular writer's motivation. And since most of us are often unaware of—or embarrassed by—competitive urges, it is difficult to rely on students' retrospective accounts. For example, when I told Maura I was thinking of studying competition in my course, she said, "It's funny that I wrote about that field hockey stuff because I'm not a competitive person."

My own approach was fairly simple and straightforward: I interviewed my students. "Do you feel competitive with other students in this course? with anyone in particular? What is happening when you are feeling this way? Does my behavior contribute to your competitive feelings in any way? Do you feel competitive in the same ways in your other classes?" I focused only on those moments when a student's actions or emotions—anxiety, ambition, anger, satisfaction—could be identified as a direct result of comparing himself to his peers. In other words, since a student might feel tense, anxious, or ambitious for a number of reasons unrelated to competition, I did not automatically identify all examples of writing apprehension or all evidence of academic ambition as competitive behavior. Also, since the focus of the study was peer competition, I did not include instances in which a student saw himself competing against some abstract standard, against a teacher, or even in some sense against himself. What interested me were those cases in which a student perceived other students as rivals.

Although I was primarily interested in how students interacted with each other around this issue, I felt some self-study was essential. To determine what role I played in this process, I kept a journal in which I identified classroom situations during which I was aware of acting either to provoke competitive feelings and motivation in the students (e.g., lavishly praising a hardworking student in front of a less diligent student or announcing that I would publish a limited collection of student essays to be used as a text for next year's class) or to neutralize them (e.g., telling students that the primary purpose of writing is discovery and self-knowledge or consciously deciding not to praise a student in public because it might make other students anxious).

Of course, like all self-respecting, process-oriented, nonauthoritarian composition teachers, I began this study believing that the atmosphere in my classroom is supportive, even nurturing. After all, I use procedures that are designed, at least in part, to neutralize direct competition between students: I emphasize personal voice, experimentation, and revision; I delay evaluation until the end of the course, usually responding to student writing in individual conferences; although I occasionally require students to try to write on a particular topic or in a particular mode, I generally give them the freedom to work on their own topics at their own pace. Much class time is devoted to small-group discussions of drafts in progress, and students may choose to do some of their writing collaboratively. At the end of the semester all students have to assemble a portfolio that they feel demonstrates the quality, quantity, and range of writing they have produced and they have to identify their three best pieces of writing.

But, at the same time, I also believe—and in this way, too, I am like all self-respecting process teachers—that this "noncompetitive" atmosphere makes my course unique. In other words, I often remind myself that my course exists within a college that uses traditional teaching and evaluation techniques, ones that typically emphasize competition: for example, the administration pressures the faculty to resist grade inflation by strongly recommending that classes be evaluated according to a rigid "curve"; there is a reliance in most classes on frequent "objective" quizzes and exams; and the registrar regularly distributes information on GPA and class rank. But that is not the only reason I congratulate myself on bucking the system. Or, to put it another way, that is not the only system I think I am bucking: after all, the college exists within a political, economic, and cultural system that generally accepts the notion that individuals must compete for scarce and limited resources.

The results? What is the nature of competition in a process writing course? In one sense it's fairly straightforward:

Walt: In every course students want good grades and there are always a limited number of good grades. We all know that. There is no doubt in my mind that you are not going to give 20 A's. There is no doubt in my mind that you are not going to give 10 A's and 10 B's. It's just not going to happen. Almost everyone comes to college thinking he is a B or better, but the professors have to give a certain number of C's. So if you want a good grade—in any course—you have to do better than most of the other students in the class.

This perception—that good grades are a limited resource allocated not on need but on relative performance—seems to exist across the curriculum. But that may be where the similarity between competition in process writing courses and competition in more traditional courses ends. What I learned is that our efforts to neutralize competition between writing students do not eliminate that competition but rather complicate it. In fact the most intense competition occurs around three of the fundamental methods of most process writing teaching: (1) the development of an individualized curriculum; (2) the use of untraditional or qualitative assessment measures; and, (3) the use of peer workshop methods.

Competition and the Individualized Curriculum

Every single student I interviewed pointed out immediately one way in which competition in my class was different from competition in their other courses. In a traditional course, they explained, it was relatively easy to tell how the competition worked and who they were competing against.

Polly: Whenever you have the same assignment as everyone else, it puts more pressure on you because you feel like you're being compared to each other. So if I take an exam in bio, it almost feels like an IQ test because we are all being graded on the exact same thing. Or when I hand in a paper in sociology I think, "I hope mine is on the top so she won't be sick of reading about this" or "I hope mine is on the bottom so she sees how it's better than the others." Because we all have to write on the same thing and I want mine to stand out. But in your class the papers are usually totally different from each other. Sometimes it's almost like you're taking a different course.

This isn't surprising. Perhaps the trademark of any process writing course is the tremendous degree of freedom and responsibility it gives students to develop their own materials and methods (see, for example, William Clark's "How to Completely Individualize a Writing Program"). The idea is to treat each student writer as unique, as an individual. Therefore, students are free to choose their own topics, even to write in a particular genre or mode of discourse. In my course, this sense of choice and individuation is particularly intense because I almost never read a batch of essays at once, preferring instead to respond to each essay when the student brings it in to a conference. The illusion, then, is that a student is competing only against herself, that is, against her own standards or perhaps against what the student takes to be her teacher's standards. Or put another way: since the student is in some sense constructing her own curriculum, she does not need to worry excessively about how her work compares with her classmates'.

But while almost every student noted this relative lack of standardization, the responses to it varied widely. Although a number of students commented that they resented the competition in courses with standardized assignments, many complained at the same time that they suffered from the lack of comparison in my class:

Nick: In a writing course it is very hard to know where you stand. You have different topics and sometimes even different time allotments. That makes it hard. I think the more you can see what you're up against, what other people are doing, the more you try to improve yourself. It is hard to try to compare yourself with yourself. So you have to find people doing something sort of like you're doing and compare yourself with them.

A number of students tied their degree of motivation in a course directly to the degree of competition. So if these students could not identify a clear point of comparison or a clear competitor, many found that their work actually suffered:

Polly: In one way you write worse in sociology because you're not free to write about what you want to write about. But I think overall you write better because you know everyone is writing about the same thing so you want to make yours as good as it can be. But if you're writing about your relationship with your father, yours is the only one that the teacher will read, so you probably won't push yourself as hard.

Other students pointed out that to succeed in a course they need to choose a designated rival, almost the way a marathoner might choose to run on the heels of an established runner. But in a process writing course, this is tough to do, as Walt explained:

Take biology, this semester in bio-chem. Like with my lab partner. She's the smartest person in class and so I gauge my performance against hers. She got a 98 on the midterm; I got a 92. That's the person that I'm in competition with. We'll be doing a lab together and she'll pick out my errors, I'll pick out her errors, and we're so far above the rest of the class that you just keep trying. She knows that I'm . . . there, just behind her. And I know that she's still doing better than me. So I keep trying to catch up and that really helps my work. Now I think everyone in your class is trying to scope out the so-called brain, the smartest student, to know what you want and also how to evaluate our own performance against the brain's. But in your class scoping out who is the brain is almost impossible.

To some extent, these students seemed surprised when they suddenly realized that the course was competitive after all, almost as if they had been lulled by the individualized curriculum into thinking that they would not be compared with their classmates. Walt said that he did not think about being in direct competition with his peers until the due date for the portfolio approached. Maura said she became aware that they were all being compared whenever a student volunteered to read a draft of an essay to the whole class ("When Paul read his the other day and I heard the way it was written, especially the vocabulary, I thought, 'Oh, oh, I'm in trouble' "). Polly, on the other hand, felt competitive whenever she heard other students' topics. If a classmate was writing on the same topic that she had chosen, she panicked because she "felt like the other person would probably have a better grip on it," but if a classmate was working on a different topic, she panicked even more. ("I mean I'm writing about problems with my roommate; Walt is writing about defusing a bomb that could have blown up a whole air force base. Which one is going to get a better grade?")

While these students seemed surprised by these competitive moments, they were not resentful. In fact, most suggested that they needed less competition and moments of comparison than they found in traditional courses but more than they found in my class:

Maura: It's good that we are not being compared in here all the time. Then people just say, "Forget it. I don't even want to deal with it." That's how I get in humanities and also in psychology. You get this feeling that you're being judged and watched and sometimes you can't take it. You get sick of being compared every second. So I sometimes just blow it off. I think, "I just don't care at all anymore." But in here? I would say there should be more situations where people have to compare themselves with the rest of the class, to try to do better. It helps you focus.

But how much comparison is too much? Or put another way: at what point in the process does comparison inhibit the writer and at what point does it motivate him? Nick's explanation is typical:

I think competition is very bad at the beginning of the writing process because it cuts off my creativity, especially during brainstorming. If I get competitive at the beginning I get worried about what I should write for you rather than what I should write for myself, so I try not to think about what other people are doing. But as it gets towards the end, I think it's really good if you're pushing yourself to be the best. It keeps me editing and getting on with the work.

In the end I realized it is not just the curriculum that is highly individualized; so are the students, each of whom brings a different set of goals and strategies to competitive situations:

Maura: It guess it would help if I could compare myself with someone in this class. But I don't think I really need to. The reason I am trying so hard, writing so many drafts, is because I have to do better than my brother. He's at another college and is just one year ahead of me. We both have always done well in school and we always put our grades up on the refrigerator. Well, he got a 3.7 GPA. I think I did pretty well for the first semester, a 3.3 here is really good. But there is absolutely no way that I am going to have the lower grades on the refrigerator next time. So I just keep writing.

Competition and Untraditional Assessment Measures

Most process teachers try to deemphasize grades—by not grading rough drafts, by taking the entire writing process into account during evaluation, by giving students some role in choosing what work should be graded, and by telling students that a writing course is as much about process as product. But we should not kid ourselves: although we talk about decentering authority and we work at demystifying grades, our students are competing in a larger culture that emphasizes—even depends on—hierarchal evaluation. What is different in a process writing course is the extent to which the students' desire for a good grade makes them feel dependent on gaining the teacher's approval. Because our assessment methods seem more qualitative than those used in most other courses and because students are often dealing with highly personal topics, some students view grades and the teacher's approval in a process writing course as identical:

Polly: I think students worry all the time what a teacher thinks, about a teacher's approval, but it's really because we want the grade. It's like a dog race around here to get grades in most classes. In most courses, no one cares about the learning, just getting the higher grade. So trying to get on a teacher's good side is really important. But it's especially important in a writing class. In a bio or pscyh course you answer the questions on the exam; they are right or wrong and you get that grade. What the teacher thinks about you isn't as important. But as far as writing a paper, how the teacher approaches it and how you write it are going to determine your grade, and that is less objective. Honestly, if you think the teacher hates you, it is really hard to write.

No matter how much we want to claim that our evaluation of their essays is somehow objective or unbiased, most students seem to understand and accept our subjectivity as a given. And so it becomes extremely important to them that we approve of what they are doing or, perhaps more to the point, that we approve of what they are doing at least as much as we approve of their classmates' efforts. That's why so many students spend a great deal of time and energy comparing their own relationship with the teacher with the relationship that the teacher has with their classmates:

Polly: I admit that I feel really competitive with people in the class, especially Ben. And I'm not the only one. I've talked with Maura about this because we live on the same floor. I also think that the guys in the class feel the exact same way. It is almost as if he has an edge in the class because he's older and so he can relate to you better. It's like everything he writes, we all think we could never write as well because we don't have all that experience so we could never talk about the same things in our essays or in class with you.

Polly not only resents Ben's cocky attitude ("I felt this from the first day, from the first time I heard him talk, from the times when he would argue with the guys in the class"), she also resents the relationship that she perceives he has with me ("I almost had the feeling that he thinks that no one in the class has the intelligence to keep up with you, like we'd have nothing to say to you if we bumped into you at the coffee shop or post office"). Polly, like most of the others I interviewed, seemed to be keeping close tabs on the student-teacher relationships in each of her classes, particularly the ones with essays to be graded. To a certain extent students seem to blame teachers for creating these competitive feelings, for making students feel dependent on our approval. Rachel repeatedly cited my role in this:

Like when you told Tina that she did a really great job on that in-class assignment where you asked us to write about the same experience in three different ways. Some people might say, "Good, I can go see Tina. She knows what's going on in here." Or some people might say, "Tina—what a jerk!" Someone in the class will go read Tina's paper and say, "Now finally I get it." But the others would say, "Forget it. I won't even try. I can never be like her and he obviously really likes her. I can never be like her, so why bother?"

As much as my students might resent a teacher for having pets or for playing one student off against another, they resent even more strongly classmates who compete unfairly for a teacher's approval. Clearly this competition is governed by peer values and unwritten rules. To violate these rules—to compete too aggressively or obsequiously—for a teacher's approval is to risk alienating classmates, risk being labeled a "brownnoser" or "kiss-up." Or to put it another way: while students are competing for teacher approval, they are also competing for peer respect, and these two competitive endeavors are often in conflict. For example, Polly felt that Ben, a nontraditional student, was being "completely unfair" in his attempt to win my good favor by constantly bringing up things he shared with me—by virtue of his age and experience—that the others could not possibly share.

As she pointed out, she wasn't the only one who felt that way: it was reasonable, she said, for students to compete for my approval and attention, but "they shouldn't be doing it at the other students' expense."

What else was seen as unfair competition? Some students complained about classmates who sought and received what they considered too much extra help with essays:

Rachel: We all want to do well and to be on good terms with the teacher but there is almost a group consensus in a way as to what is fair and what isn't. Like a student going to talk to a professor ten times about a paper or talking to ten different professors about a paper. That's unfair. That person has stepped out and gone over and above the assignment. It would be different at a school like Cornell where the competition is to do as well as you can but here the competition is to get by with the least effort possible. I bet at Cornell if you heard that someone went to twelve teachers it would be really "up there," respected, and you would think, "Then I'm going to thirteen." But here we all snicker and think that the person who does it is horrible.

By definition, competition is directly related to scarcity, to the effort to win a limited resource. But when I pointed out to Rachel that I had never told students that there was a limit to how many times they could see me for help with a particular essay, she said:

Yeah, but the thing that's unfair about running to ten different teachers or to the same teacher ten times is that if every single person did that, then no one could do it because it's not as if the professors have time to see every paper twelve times. Professors don't have unlimited time to meet with students.

Many students seem to have a fairly clear idea of what is fair and unfair. If a classmate violates the code, she might be criticized, even ostracized. Many students, including Rachel, were critical of classmates who tried too aggressively to please a teacher by hoarding class time:

I've been in classes where we are being graded on class discussion and two or three people just take over the class and then what do you do? You're not going to interrupt. Those students weren't very popular, I'll tell you that. And those are probably the same people who go to ten professors, who just push themselves up to the top. In a lot of cases it isn't quality of participation that counts with a teacher and it's too bad because there are always people who have good things to say who can't get a word in edgewise. I blame the teacher for not controlling the class in a fair way but also I blame the students who are doing that.

Many of these students put themselves in a nearly impossible competitive situation. Since they want their teacher to be a fair and sympathetic evaluator of their essays, they need to compete for his attention and approval; but if they compete too aggressively, they feel embarrassed in front of their peers. (More on that in the next chapter.) And so these students spend much of their time in the writing class consciously holding back and, at the same time, glancing over their shoulders to make sure that everyone else is holding back, too.

Of course, some students, just like some universities, are less ambivalently competitive than others. Walt, another nontraditional student, told me that he was less influenced by peer pressure than the traditional undergraduates:

> I find myself in more competition in some ways and in less in other ways because I've come back to school after a number of years rather than coming straight to a composition class as an eighteen-year-old high school kid. I know some of the other students might think I'm a brownnoser or something but to tell you the truth, I don't care. Freshmen don't really know what it's like outside, so they're just going along trying to get by, trying to fit in. But I've worked real jobs, I was in the air force for three years and I was a SAAB mechanic for four more—so I know what it's like out there and I want to do a lot more than just get by.

Of course, none of these issues are unique to process courses or even to composition. Students must always negotiate the perilous borders between the teacher's approval, peer respect, and sense of self. But process courses seem to bring these issues to the front in a particularly intense way, as this comment by Rachel indicates:

> The whole thing is really complicated in a writing course. And when you are competing with your friends there is emotion involved. It's much more complicated. You don't want to jeopardize the friendship, so you don't want to do worse or better than they do. It just seems like there are a lot of really subtle rules about competition and it's hard to figure them out. I think the rules really depend on the class, though. If you're in a big class and you don't know anyone and it is all based on test grades, not on what the teacher thinks, then you just do the best you can do. I think I do best when there is no direct competition, stuff with your friends. Then I can try my hardest without worrying about other people's feelings.

So while these issues do exist in all courses, we raise the stakes; first, by asking students to write about what they really feel and think, and second, by using assessment measures that are not "objective," measures that make students believe that our approval is a significant, perhaps a crucial, part of evaluation. Given those factors, it's not surprising that competition in composition makes students examine their own basic values:

Rachel: The people I feel competitive with in your class are the students that I was talking about who go to ten different professors. They're the ones who break the competition rules in my opinion. Are they such good students because they get so much extra help? Or do they go find extra help because they are good students? I'm sure that most people think they get good grades in writing because they do that sort of thing and they are not the most popular people. But whenever you see something like this in the movies, you see ten years later and they're the ones who end up to be the presidents of the companies and the rest of us who spent our time trying to be friends end up pumping gas. They always win by doing that, but still people don't want to do it.

Competition and the Peer Workshop

At the center of most process classes is some form of peer response or workshop. The idea is to neutralize the teacher's authority as critic and evaluator, to give students some sense of a wider audience, and to create a small community of writers. Once again, it is tempting to assume that peer response groups reduce the usual competitive relationships in classes by linking students in cooperative activities. But since process courses provide students with relatively few chances *besides* peer workshops to compare themselves with their classmates, these interactions can become a highly charged source of competition. In fact, many of my students pointed out that just reading or listening to another student's essay often triggered strong competitive feelings. Maura's comment is typical:

> For me the first time I personally felt competitive towards the other students was probably when we had to read our first papers out loud. I felt like my paper had to be up to par with the other students. I think in a way this helped my paper. I didn't want to sound like a total idiot in front of everyone, so I took time, revised my paper, and finally came up with something that I could be proud of. So it actually helped.

But it is not just reading their own writing in workshop that creates feelings of competition; it is also listening and reading essays by other students. Almost every student I interviewed acknowledged a degree of anxiety and envy when they heard or read an outstanding essay by a classmate. But it is significant that most of these students found these competitive moments helped rather than hindered their own writing by giving them incentive, ideas, even strategies, for their own essays.

The corollary, of course, is that many students feel a certain relief, even satisfaction, when they came across a relatively weak peer essay:

Polly: I guess I feel relieved in a way when I read a bad essay [by one of my classmates]. But I'd only hope the other papers would be bad if I'm having a really hard time myself. Especially when the other people are my friends. If I hear a paper that is awful, then I feel bad for the student. But if someone reads a really good one, and you knew that yours was going to be read by that same teacher, it adds a lot of pressure. I wouldn't hope that people I knew would fail, ever. But if I don't like the people very much, then I do feel differently and hope they would do poorly so it would help me.

Given the commitment that most process teachers have to creating a supportive community of writers, this may seem disheartening news. But most students—as Walt explains—see a certain logic and justification to their response:

> I do feel better to hear papers that aren't so great. I feel that way with some people more than others. You've been stressing that we have a lot of responsibility and freedom in the course . . . well, a lot of people don't always show up for class on a regular basis or work very hard on their drafts for workshop. So I don't feel bad if they write a bad essay; in fact I feel good. If they don't want to put in the time or effort or they don't even remember to bring in drafts when we are reading each other's paper, then they deserve to do poorly.

The real issue here is not so much how a student feels in a peer response group when listening to a weak essay but rather how she acts in this situation. A number of students, including Polly, admitted that they feel terribly conflicted in these situations:

> I'm not sure if I would want to help someone. It depends. This sounds horrible, I know. But I'm not sure; it depends if it was a friend. And I don't know if it is even my place to tell them. I think every case is different. I don't know.

Others, however, do know how they behave when they are working in a group with a weak writer: they hold back their comments. In fact, most have given the matter enough thought to tell me the extent to which they hold back:

Nick: I'm probably selfish but I wouldn't want to bring someone up to an A. Maybe a B but definitely not up to an A—if I thought I might be able to get an A. I don't know if it's selfish or if it's just that I think people should do their own work. But I wouldn't help too much.

Walt: If I noticed a problem with someone's essay, I'd probably tell them what I thought they ought to change to make it better. But the real question is: would a student ever give another student enough help to bring it up to his speed? I don't think I'd do that. You might say to the person, "You're going about it wrong and here's a way to go about it." But to go further than that in the process, no, I wouldn't do that. The student would then be judged and graded based on what you thought, not what he thought. You help a little bit and you never try to mess up someone's essay, but more often than not you don't want to help them too much because you don't want to bring someone else's paper up to your pace.

Polly: I am sort of moody so it depends on how I feel I did. If I feel like I have done a really good job on my paper, then reading someone else's paper won't bother me. In fact I'll try to help them. But if I feel insecure about the job I did, then reading someone else's will just get me nervous. And I won't help them. I mean if theirs is better I'll probably be looking for them to help me with mine.

I have often heard colleagues say that peer reviewers hold back because they lack confidence or because they don't want to hurt their classmates' feelings—and that certainly happens—but I now realize that many hold back to protect their own interests. Before you judge any of them too harshly, listen to the question Walt posed for me:

> I would not want to give other students anything they couldn't do on their own. If you help someone more than they could help themselves, then it's like plagiarism. You're giving them their ideas, your ideas, and you're imposing yourself on their paper and their grade. You also don't want to help them more than you can help yourself either. I know how that sounds but, I mean, think about it. Let's say you were writing a grant and someone else was too, trying for the exact same grant. Sure, you might help him, but would you help him so much that it might end up better than yours?

Implications

So what does all of this mean for composition teachers? First, it means that we need to move beyond the simplistic notion that collaborative or process classrooms are not competitive. These are not either/or choices: people often compete in cooperative situations and cooperate in competitive ones. Just because we say that we are engaged in "collaborative learning" does not mean that our students are always behaving collaboratively. In fact, these preliminary results suggest an ironic possibility about process classrooms: because process teachers rely on untraditional assessment measures, because they ask students to write on subjects in which they have a great personal investment, and most of all because they drive competition underground, students may actually be most competitive in process writing classes.

Process classrooms exist within competitive environments, are taken by competitive students, and believe it or not are often taught by competitive teachers. All of which means that we need to move beyond a second simplistic notion: that competition is always a negative force for writers. The students I interviewed had all sorts of reasons for supporting competition in a writing course. "It helps me focus." "It makes me try harder." "It gives me something to shoot for." At the same time, they all felt that at certain moments competitive feelings and behavior hurt their writing and made them want to give up in frustration or even fear. So while it seems wrong to encourage or allow cutthroat competition in our classes, it also seems a mistake to try to eliminate what seems to be healthy or productive competition. My hypothesis—and I admit this is based as much on my own experience and on conversations with colleagues as it is on my discussions with students—is that writers work best when they can establish a productive level of competition; by productive I mean not so high that writers give up in frustration but not so low that they ignore it as an incentive.

Third, we need to ask what role we play in establishing or modulating this level. A significant one. Again and again students pointed out to me ways in which I was contributing to their competitive struggles. Some of these ways were systematic—I individualized the curriculum, eschewed "objective" testing, and required peer workshops—but others were quirky and seemingly random: I called on Lisa to read more times than I called on Denise; I let Ken schedule so many individual conferences; I laughed harder at Emily's satiric piece about the uselessness of physics than I did at Ray's modest proposal for solving the problem of homelessness; and who knows what else? Clearly we can't eliminate competition, but we can pay more attention to how our actions and inactions might affect our students and then adjust in ways that are productive for them as writers and as people.

Fourth, and this issue lurks at the edges of this entire study, we need to ask in what ways gender shapes competition. The assumption of many people undertaking composition studies is that competition is primarily negative and primarily male. (See, for example, Charles Schuster's or Susan Miller's comments on this in *The Politics of Writing Instruction: Postsecondary*). Since I am limited by my own male perspective and since I have looked at such a small sample size, I obviously can't make any conclusive statements about gender and competition in composition. Still, for what it is worth, let me offer one speculative conclusion: while it is true that the females I interviewed seemed more uncomfortable, more ambivalent, about their competitive feelings than the males seemed about theirs, the intensity and frequency of those feelings were just as strong.

And here I think process teachers and feminist theorists share a common perspective and concern: just as most process teachers are tempted to deny or reject competition out of hand, most academic feminists seek to replace the hegemonic dependency on competition with a more supportive and equitable system, a "sisterhood" or "web." Fortunately, that desire has not kept some feminist writers from discussing and facing fundamental problems in this area. Are women naturally less competitive than men? Do women compete differently against men than they do against other women? How can women deal with the fact that our society and educational system is basically competitive?

While most feminists do posit alternate models to the competitive, hierarchal educational system (see, for example, *Women's Ways of Knowing* Belenky et al.), others point out at the same time that whether women would behave competitively if men did not exist or if resources were not scarce are moot questions. As Evelyn Keller and Helene Moglen argue, academic women are competitive because our classrooms exist within a society in which there are limited resources and hierarchal structures. This is true for everyone in the academy, but competition creates special problems for feminists—and for process writing teachers—because it runs counter to images these groups have of themselves and their mission. Valerie Miner, a feminist novelist, raises the crucial questions about these issues:

> Why do I sometimes feel a twinge when another women succeeds? Why do I occasionally become livid? Shouldn't I feel gratified when any of my sisters does well? Isn't feminism antithetical to competition? (183)

While Miner is clearly bothered by cutthroat competition, she argues that for several reasons women need to acknowledge the inevitable and even positive aspects of competition: the division of scarce resources always depends to some extent on competition; competitive urges sometimes lead to creative breakthroughs; and "cooperative competition . . . can provoke us to go deeper emotionally, to play more boldly with forms" (193).

Miner's point—that the issue is not whether we feel competitive urges but rather what we do with those urges—is crucial because it moves beyond the simplistic identification of competition as inherently negative. This move may be as difficult for process writing teachers as it has been for feminists—and for many of the same reasons: we too like to believe that we are providing an alternative to hegemonic politics, values, and discourse. By emphasizing process, collaboration, and social construction, we too like to think that we have successfully moved beyond rigid guidelines and hierarchies.

But we have come to this position without paying any attention to how competition actually functions in process classrooms. And it is here that Miner's work as a feminist provides direction for those of us who teach writing:

> The first step toward understanding is to acknowledge the existence of competition in our family lives and in our public spheres. It is painful to admit the deep rivalries we have had with sisters and mothers, just as it is embarrassing to point to our competition with other women in workplaces, neighborhoods, and political groups. If we could stop feeling defensive and fearful long enough to consider how we compete not only for money but also for attention and affection and righteousness, we might be better able to eliminate the negative elements of competitiveness from our lives. (1–2)

Finally, if there are directions for future research here, I hope they will include studying ourselves as well as our students. In other words, if we really want to understand how competition functions in our classrooms, we need to demystify it—for them and for ourselves. And that means we have to look at our own competitive urges. This is never easy, so let me try to get the ball rolling: a few summers ago, I took, at the University of New Hampshire, a course called Writing for Teachers. Don Murray, one of the founders of the writing process movement, was the teacher and he went out of his way to make us comfortable. He told us the first day, "We will learn together. This will be fun." And this: "As far as I'm concerned, you all have A's in this course and you'd have to do a lot to convince me otherwise." Since most of the teachers in the course were not taking it for graduate credit, the grade shouldn't have mattered much anyway.

But although Murray did all the right things to make us feel comfortable, I wasn't comfortable. I was intense; anxious, obsessed not only with the writing but also with everyone else's writing, with Murray's responses to my writing and with his responses to my classmates' writing. The other day, I went back and read my journal during that period. In one entry I complain about my fellow students who were having an easier time writing than I was:

> July 7: I'm having a hard time figuring out where to go next with my story. I keep trying to plot it out, to figure out what should happen, but the people in my small group keep telling me to relax, to do what they are doing—letting the story develop itself. Now I was suspicious enough when I read all those quotes by Fitzgerald and Faulkner like "I don't know where my characters are taking me. I follow them around with a notebook and jot down what they are saying," but I am doubly suspicious when people in this class claim that is what their process is like, who say, "I can't wait to get back

to my desk to find out what my characters are doing now." Come on. Maybe it's I'm jealous, but I just don't believe all this stuff. Writing is hard work, deliberate work. This all seems to me like the emperor's new clothes.

In another entry I admit that I am jealous of the attention and approval Murray was giving my classmates:

> August 5: I believe in this process approach. I believe in peer response groups. And I believe that in some ways we have become a community of writers this summer, but I'm starting to go nuts during the workshop time in class: I often wait for my turn like a three-year-old. (What about me? I've talked enough about your story. What do you think of my story?) And that's not all: when Don tells Gail that her writing on the sawmill is just right, like a first draft, but beautifully written, and he tells Sharon that he can't wait to see her next draft and tells Esther how well her revision works and tells Rich that his story ought to be published and tells Tom that he has one of the strongest voices he has ever read, all I can think about is, "What does he think about my story? Is my story good?"

So what was going on? First, I think it's clear that I wanted desperately for Don Murray to like me and to like my writing. That part makes sense: I had first become attracted to process teaching through Murray's *A Writer Teaches Writing* and had several times used *Write to Learn* as a textbook. But the surprising and embarrassing part is that I wanted Murray to like me and my writing as much or more than he liked my classmates and their work.

If you are one of those people who really don't feel competitive in this way, I envy you. I'm competitive with you even about that. And it may be that the reasons for my own intense competitive feelings are hidden in places only my therapist can help me get. But after listening to student after student talk about competition, my suspicion is that what I was feeling that summer was not all that different from what most of them feel in process writing courses. This does not mean that we should let competition run wild in our classes or that we should give up on collaboration, peer workshops, or nontraditional assessment. But if we want to understand and establish productive writing relationships, maybe it is time to give up something: talking about these issues in such idealistic and, even worse, moralistic language that we fail to recognize our students or ourselves.

Chapter Seven

Modeling: The Power of Identification and the Identification of Power

Stan was struggling in my class. Or at least I was struggling with him. He wrote his first essay on reverse discrimination, focusing on "the unfair advantages that blacks receive when they apply to college," "the drain on society caused by all the blacks on welfare," and the fact that "we would never even be considering a national holiday for someone like Martin Luther King if he had not been black." I wasn't sure if the essay was as poorly written and organized as it seemed, or if I just was focusing on the problems because the ideas were repugnant to me. In our conferences, I pushed him to challenge his own assumptions; I suggested that his tone might turn off some readers; I asked him if he thought he needed to do some research. He passively resisted everything I tried: clearly these were ideas he had thought about and talked about before. He was confident about his evidence ("Martin Luther King had affairs, plagiarized his law school papers, and told blacks to break the law. Why should we honor someone like that?") and he was suspicious of my political stance ("So you don't agree with any of this, do you?"). Finally, out of frustration, I said, "Maybe I'm being overly critical. Why don't you read this one in class today and see what other people think?"

As soon as I'd said it, I knew the risk. In the best-case scenario, the other students would raise the ethical, political, and rhetorical questions about Stan's arguments that I wanted them to raise. And, of course, it would be much more effective if his discriminatory positions were exposed and challenged by his peers rather than by me. But I've taught long enough to know that what I hope students will say, what I want them to say, is not necessarily what gets said.

In some classes this has been a real problem for me; I once taught an advanced composition course in which the small-group and whole-class peer review sessions not only failed to support my suggestions, they aggressively contradicted them. "What if you tried so and so?" I would cautiously suggest to a student. "I wouldn't change a thing," someone else would counter. "It would ruin the whole effect you're trying for. Your piece is perfect the way it is." I'd look around the room at the nodding faces and mumble a conciliatory statement that belied the anger I felt.

And, in fact, the day Stan read his essay turned out to be a difficult one for me. I said nothing at first, hoping for the resistance, the cultural critique, to emerge. Although several students disagreed with his assessment of King and a few raised questions about specific aspects of his argument, they were not aggressive or confident in their criticism. In fact, most of the students in my almost-all-white, almost-all-middle-class class either supported Stan's argument or stayed quiet. I suspected that many must have disagreed with some of Stan's arguments but were intimidated by his aggressive positions and effect. "You said it's good to take a strong position in an essay, didn't you?" he said to me during the discussion. "Isn't that what I'm doing in this essay?"

Still I held back, waiting and hoping that one of Stan's classmates would tell him strong positions were one thing and racism was another, that the fact that we would not be honoring King if he were not black was actually the point, and that the welfare bashing in Stan's essay played on dangerous stereotypes. But all along I knew that it was unfair to put them on the spot by asking them to say what I wanted said. So I tried to make my point through some pointed questions: "Don't you think some of your audience might find your positions offensive? Wouldn't it make more sense to present a more balanced view?" But I am no Socrates and Stan was no easy target. Finally, since no one had offered a strong counterstatement and since I worried that my own neutral, non-political questions might be interpreted as agreement or indifference, I finally launched into an impromptu, free-form, much-too-long-and-angry lecture about racism, bigotry, and middle-class indifference in America.

Actually, the idea that a productive peer critique or dialectic should or will develop in writing workshops is based on all sorts of questionable assumptions—that a true diversity of opinion, knowledge, and perspective exists in our classes; that students are willing to challenge one another's political opinions and to critique one another's rhetorical ability; that, in short, students have the ability to teach one another through direct debate and instruction.

These assumptions do sometimes turn out to be true. I have seen students learn from one another in peer-editing sessions and I have occasionally had lively political debates in my classes. But these lively debates rarely focus on the writing of one of the members of the class; and the problem of students' not challenging one another, not saying what we hope they will say about another student's paper, is not limited to political or controversial topics. In many ways the problem of passivity and detachment is even more common with rhetorical questions. Quite simply, peer editors often do not suggest what we think is needed. This may be because they do not want to violate an unwritten pact that makes them allies against us, the common enemy, or—as Tom Newkirk has suggested in his study of peer response groups ("Direction")—it may be because students have different values, tastes, and criteria for assessment than we do.

Still, as we all know from watching adolescents in general and our own students in particular, they influence and teach one another in all sorts of ways and situations. How else can we explain how teenagers in the same social group all seem to know what music to listen to, what kind of clothes to wear, what talk to talk, even what walk to walk? Clearly they don't attend peer workshops on these topics. Often they don't even discuss these issues directly. But through observing and modeling, they figure out values, expectations, conventions, strategies.

The same thing happens when it comes to writing. The problem is that some of the values, expectations, conventions, and strategies they gain through modeling are not the ones we would want them to learn (more on that later in this chapter). But others, like the ones Isabelle taught my class, are exactly the ones I had tried and failed to teach during my run-in with Stan. Isabelle, the daughter of a white father and a black mother, said nothing when Stan read his Martin Luther King essay, but a few weeks later she agreed to read aloud her own essay on race relations in America. In that essay she wrote about the rage she felt at white bigots but also about the shame she felt the day her mother asked her why she had no close black friends.

> Am I insulting my mother by not having black friends? I have Jewish, Asian, Hispanic, and white friends, so why have I excluded blacks from that circle? Am I secretly racist myself? Am I denying the darker side of myself? Am I afraid in America to be black? These are all questions I can't answer. I am afraid to answer.
> Then again why should I have to?

No one said much after Isabelle read her essay. And I was not sure what anyone had learned about writing or race relations from it. But later that week, Ted brought in an essay about a school hockey game he had played, about how his father had pushed him to "be aggressive out there every second," about how he became increasingly physical and confrontational in the game until he provoked a violent fight. As soon as I started reading that essay, I sensed that Ted's voice in this essay was different from his voice in his earlier pieces; he seemed more intense, more focused. And then I came to this paragraph:

> Would I have acted differently if my father had not spoken to me before the game? Was rushing the net my own decision or was I obeying my father subconsciously? If I was playing for my father, how many others were playing for their father? Why did we feel we had to?

I knew where Ted had found that voice, that tone, that rhetorical style. I knew it wasn't from me and I knew that no one had suggested it directly. I had no trouble seeing how Isabelle had influenced, no, taught him to write like that. Taught him that it was OK to write about problems with parents, that it was powerful to discuss doubts as well as beliefs, and that rhetorical questions could be more effective than declarative statements. And I was even more convinced that Isabelle's lesson had affected the whole class when Henry soon brought in an essay about the time he defied his mother's warning about jumping his dirtbike off a small cliff. The experience ended with a broken ankle; the essay ended with that familiar list of rhetorical questions. By the end of the term, I began calling this form "an Isabelle paper."

But this recognition—that students can teach one another in powerful ways—suddenly raises a pentad of questions: Who in the class is doing most of the teaching? What exactly are the other students learning? When is this teaching most likely to occur? Where is it most likely to occur? And why am I suddenly writing in rhetorical questions?

Identification

I should not have been surprised that so many of my students began writing "Isabelle papers," just as I should not have been surprised the next semester when the same thing happened again: this time everyone wrote "Carolyn essays" (though it is a form that John McPhee has also used a few times and identified as a "contrapunctual time" structure), a literary form in which the writer moves back and forth between chronological narrative of a specific event (a tennis match, a drive to school, a political campaign) and more random thoughts that are only tangentially related to the narrative action. I should not have been surprised because I had seen it so many times before—in my daughter's first-grade classroom, where riddle books, mystery stories, or pop-up books would pop up, sweep through the entire class, and then disappear to be replaced by the new hot genre the next week.

And I should not have been surprised because it's so logical—and so deeply rooted in the teaching and study of writing. Modeling and identification are both familiar terms and age-old research topics for rhetoricians. Quintilian and others urged the use of imitation to teach writing, and composition specialists have long hoped that students can gain a certain fluency and rhetorical sophistication by being exposed to essays such as Orwell's "Shooting an Elephant" or E. B. White's "Once More to the Lake." And it could be argued that *identification*—as the term is used by writers such as Kenneth Burke and Chaim Perelman—is the key to the New Rhetoric.

However, imitation, like the modes of discourse or sentence combining, has fallen on such hard times that most writing teachers have become reluctant to ask students to copy prose models. But even when we don't ask, students do it anyway. And they imitate not only prose styles but—and this is what interests me most—they also imitate styles of composing and attitudes toward writing. Robert Brooks, in his study "Modeling a Writer's Identity," explains this use of *identification*:

> When a student (or any writer) successfully learns something about writing by imitation, it is by imitating another person, and not a text or a process. Writers learn to write by imitating other writers, by trying to act like writers they respect. The forms, the processes, the texts are in themselves less important as models to be imitated than the personalities or identities of the writers who produce them. (23)

As teachers we try to provide a positive model of a practicing reader and writer for our students to observe and emulate. Still, our behavior and advice is only part of the process; a student may resist seeing herself as a writer and modeling our approach to writing because of values and goals that she brings to the class or because of pressure she feels from her classmates. From our point of view, this is often problematic, because many students identify with peer product and processes that we see as negative or counterproductive. (I am not referring here to ineffective composing strategies or incorrect rules of usage, but rather to counterproductive attitudes about us as teachers or about writing in general.)

With the exception of Brooke's study on "underlife" in the writing class, there is little information about the informal and sometimes subversive (at least from our point of view) ways that students teach one another in writing courses. When we try to assess learning, our tendency is to focus on the teacher-student relationship or on the aspects of the student-student relationship that we have set up ourselves. In other words, if we consider peer relationships at all, we look at official or formal peer response groups rather than at informal peer interactions. But if we stop and think about our classrooms, we know that what we have set up, what we hope for, is never all that is really going on.

Once again, I am struck by the overwhelming complexity that a student in a process classroom faces. Should he identify with the model of a writer provided by his teacher? Or the very different one provided by his peers? While I may tell a student that writing is a deeply personal and exhilarating journey, that I want her to become obsessed with her topics, that I value commitment and process as much as achievement and product, that it may take weeks or even months to discover an essay's meaning and potential, she and her classmates may be telling one another—not so much in words but in action and inaction—that it is just not too cool to try too hard or to care too much.

In fact, in an odd twist, the competition not to be—or at least not to appear—competitive may be fiercer and more difficult than the competition to win a good grade or the teacher's approval:

Rachel: The competition to *not* try is huge actually. I think it's not cool to try too hard. There is also competition to see who can do the least amount of work and still get by, like "I only spent two hours on my essay." "So what? I only spent one hour." And also who can do your work, your essays, at the very last minute. That is a very big deal. The person who puts it off the most and sleeps the least wins. The reason you didn't sleep is not that you work so hard; it's the opposite. The reason you didn't sleep is that the assignment didn't even touch you all these weeks so now you had to do it in just one night.

One of the things that students learn from one another is how not to try, how not to think of themselves as writers. From what I gathered in my interviews on competition, peer pressure is such a powerful force that it is almost always present in a student's mind. At the same time it is often difficult to read, particularly because many students say one thing and do another.

Polly: As strange as it seems to complain about students who always come in for extra help, I kind of feel that way myself. It's unfair because we should be able to do our work without running to the teacher every day. But for me if I heard someone else in our class doing it, it might make me come see you that much, too. Because if I heard that someone in our class came to see you ten times then I would think, "I better get moving. Maybe I should write another draft. I better have him look at my essay again." It's not like I would want to but if others were getting ahead then it's more like I'd feel like I had to. But I would be embarrassed. I would hate that, you know, if people thought I was trying to get ahead by having someone else to do my work for me.

Students are aware of performing for two audiences—teachers and peers—whose values are sometimes not only different but contradictory. A few students found it relatively easy to resolve this conflict. For example, Nick told me that writing had never been his best course, that he did not expect to be one of the top students, and that if "other people want to kiss up to a teacher, that's their problem." But most sounded more like Rachel:

> As a student you feel envious of a student who is close to the teacher and who wants the teacher to know how hard she is trying but you usually look on that person in a negative way. The kind of person who is always talking up in class, trying to give the teacher the answers he wants, telling the teacher how hard he is working. You want the teacher to like you and to know your are trying but you also want to set yourself apart from those people because they look so bad to everyone.

My point here is that identification plays a huge role in a writing class but it is a complicated one. Students may be asked implicitly to identify with the role of writer as it is described and modeled by their classroom teacher or they may feel pressured (or eager) to identify with the very different role of writer as it is defined by their peers. My sense is that a combination of these different models influences the stance and performance of most of our students. The question I want to address now is, how can we get students to identify with what we take to be positive models of the student as writer? And, by extension, how can we get students to teach one another what we want them to learn?

Again, part of the answer—as I've tried to point out in the first three chapters—is to revise our relationships to one another. Vygotsky's often quoted argument about the zone of proximal development applies here. The key to teaching and learning, he argues, is not to discover what a student can accomplish alone but to discover what she can accomplish with the assistance of a more talented peer. But for this positive student-student interaction to occur, we need to establish conditions that foster it. Part of our job, then, is to set up our classroom and course in such a way that students identify with their more capable peers.

Although this is a chapter on peer relationships, I feel compelled (once again) to point out the crucial role the teacher plays in these interactions. I am not suggesting that all peer relationships are or should be controlled or influenced by the classroom teacher. In fact, many interpersonal relationships are forged simply on the basis of a mutual resistance to the teacher's authority. In other words, like siblings, students in a class have a common enemy and thus have shared experiences and interests. But if we want to develop strong, positive, and most of all productive peer relationships, it is necessary to monitor peer interactions and to try to help students build coalitions, to help each student connect with other students who can offer advice or a positive example.

Student-Authored Textbooks

I suspect there are quite a few ways to succeed at making students feel like they are writers, but I know there are a great number of ways to fail at it. One of the surefire ways to fail is to ask students to read E. B. White or Tom Wolfe or Virginia Woolf and then tell them, "Write something like this." Another doomed approach is to put students in small peer groups and then to sit back and wait for learning and teaching to take off (much more on that in the next chapter). In the rest of this chapter I want to focus primarily on one method—the publication of student writing—that offers more chance for success by helping students identify one another and themselves as writers.

There are, of course, a number of techniques that help students see their classmates as writers; for example, I often ask students to read aloud a particularly strong draft to the entire class, not so much to allow them to receive suggestions for revision but more to give them recognition for their accomplishment. Also, whenever a student essay reminds me of a published writer's essay with a similar theme, topic, rhetorical approach, I photocopy and distribute both and then try to point out those similarities. But by far the most success I have had has been using student-authored essays as a textbook in my next year's class.

The theoretical arguments that have fueled the literature/composition split—and the resulting hierarchy that places student writing at the very bottom—have been effectively exposed and deconstructed by Janet Emig and Robert Scholes, among others. And, at this point, one of the trademarks of most process classrooms is the emphasis on and respect for student writing. This respect is manifested in large part through the use of student writing as the primary or, in some rare cases, the only text in the course. The hope is that if student essays are photocopied and distributed, students will come to see their own

and their classmates work as significant; they will, in short, come to
see themselves as writers.

But while using writing from the class as a basis for discussion
is enormously useful, it alone is not enough to make students see
themselves or their peers as writers. One problem is that this technique, like freewriting, journal writing, and many other process
methods, has become so familiar in writing courses that some students fail to see the distribution of their own work as especially
significant. Second, as I learned in my research on competition,
students are often too threatened by their classmates (who they see
as their immediate rivals) to relax and learn very much from them.
In an interview on competition, Rachel told me that when I distributed an essay from a class member as an example, it created a certain
amount of tension and resentment:

> But I think it is a big difference if the teacher brings in the paper as
> an example for everyone and shows it and explains how it can help
> than if he just says, "Tina wrote the best paper. What's wrong with
> the rest of you?" I think then you just feel angry and you want to
> give up.

A better alternative, I think, is to publish essays from the course
in order to use them as the primary text in next semester's class. This
sort of classroom publishing goes further and carries more cultural
and psychological currency than a simple exchange of papers in a
workshop; the students are writing for a less immediate and thus less
demystified audience, which ironically inspires them to try harder.
There is a significant difference in writing for the student sitting at
the next desk than in writing for the student who will sit there next
year. In order to increase this sense of significance and purpose, I
encourage students to write essays that provide insight and guidance
they think future students might need. I also print the essays in an
attractive format and sell the book at the college bookstore with other
required texts.

But beyond what trying to get published does for the writer,
reading this text is the best way I know to make students see their
peers and then themselves as writers. In other words, it is the site of
the most positive peer identifications. I have long suspected this but
I decided to test it recently in an informal survey of two of my classes.
As the final question on their final exam I asked them, "What essay
that you read in this course taught you the most about writing? You
may pick an essay from the professional or student section of the
Bedford reader [Sommers and McQuade], or an essay from *Student
Voices* [the collection of essays from last semester's students], or an
essay that was written by someone in this class."

Of the forty students who responded, thirty chose an essay from *Student Voices*; five chose a professional Bedford essay; four chose an essay from a current classmate; and one chose a student Bedford writer. Why? Again I think this has more to do with the pressure of classroom dynamics and the nuances of interpersonal relationships than with rhetorical features of the writing involved. Perhaps the professional and even the *Bedford* students seemed too distant and too accomplished to really teach them what they felt they needed to learn. Perhaps their classmates seemed too close, too much like them, while the students in the previous semester's collection—the students who sat in their classroom just one semester before, the students who survived and even flourished in the difficult circumstances they now faced—seemed to represent the more accomplished peers that Vygotsky identified.

So what did they learn from these more accomplished peers? With what, in other words, did they choose to identify? Since some of the students in the reader wrote about how to write successfully in my course, many learned new strategies and heuristics.

Ann: The essay that I read that taught me the most was probably "Constructive Procrastination" from *Student Voices.* I think it was interesting and well written. I'm not saying that it taught me to procrastinate. It taught me about the thinking process one must go through before actually writing a paper. I do not totally agree with Kevin about why you should wait until the last day to finally type it up or put your final thoughts on paper. He is right that most good ideas take time to develop. His point about the thought process was great and I never really thought about it before. So, hopefully, I can start thinking like he does—as soon as I get an assignment and not wait to start thinking till the end.

Other students, such as Kim, came right out and said that the best essay was the one whose author's experience as a writer most mirrored their own:

> The essay that taught me the most was "A Long Hard Journey" by Jack Zesko for a couple of reasons. I always have a hard time figuring out what I want to say on a paper or actually how I wanted to say it. Sometimes I would ponder over things and other times it would just come to me. The reason why I liked and learned a lot through this essay was because I realized that I wasn't alone, that a lot of people have hard times too and still come out with a great paper. Jack's essay was very informative because it is exactly the type I have been trying to write all year.

And there were many other students who, like Isabelle's classmates, learned new rhetorical strategies through their identification with the authors of these essays or who, like this student, learned a new use for an old technique:

Wanda: The essay I read that taught me the most about writing was "My Addiction" by Nicki Giankaris in the *Student Voices*. It taught me that you actually can write a successful piece about a personal experience using compare and contrast. After high school I thought I'd never want to read or write another compare and contrast in my life. The author of "My Addiction" compared being in love with an addiction to drugs. I knew a lot of people in high school who had relationships like that but I never thought of it that way. I think that the author presented the story very well by explaining how it was like she was addicted to her boyfriend even though he humiliated her, stood her up, and cheated on her. No matter what he did it was hard for her to let him go. She could not help her addiction to love, just as her boyfriend could not quit his addiction to cocaine. I especially liked the ending. It was an original way to end the piece. She said that she has been straight for six months now. By this she means that she realized that her boyfriend was not worth it and that she is no longer going out with him. I wish I wrote that essay.

Sometimes students claimed they learned lessons—even something as simple or as obvious as that it is all right to use "I" in an essay—that I had tried (unsuccessfully) to teach them. But somehow coming from a peer the lesson made sense. Louise's comment is typical:

> The essay I like best in the whole course was Marisa Kathanis' "Goodbye." In it I learned what I could do with a strong opinion. I never knew you could put your own personal opinions in an essay. Marisa not only expressed her opinion, she showed it. She spoke very articulately, she backed up what she stated, and there was logic and order expressed in her paper. After reading this short essay, it made me think and I believe if a reader reads a work and the reader ponders upon any question relating directly to the work, the writer has done a great job. I felt inspired after reading "Goodbye." It made me think about an opinion I strongly had too and it made me want to write about my experience.

Because students identified so closely with the authors of these essays, many commented that they could for the first time see their own mistakes in the writing of these peer authors. In other words, they learned what not to do in an essay, as these next two comments indicate.

Allison: I found myself responding to Julie Cioici's piece "The Girls in the Mall." I think this piece taught me the most about writing: how to lose an audience and effectiveness of a paper. I thought that Julie's piece was filled with bitter generalizations, hypocritical statements, and overall irrational accusations. Throughout the essay, Cioici assumes that all girls who "hang out" in the mall are degenerates—kids who have nothing better to do than to act "prostitute-like." I didn't think that this was good writing at all. I have always thought that it was good to have as strong a tone as possible to get your reader's attention but she showed me how to turn a reader off by using such a bitter tone. Reading this taught me that although a writer most wants to attract a reader's attention—possibly by making him angry or defensive—a piece that is filled with a bitter tone, false accusations, and overgeneralizations will only *detract* from the writing. I know I've made these mistakes in the past but after reading this essay I really tried not to make them in my papers in this course.

Michelle: I would choose "Goodbye: Leaving the Church" by Marisa Kathanis. Marisa's paper deals with some harsh feelings. She brings her feelings into the text, which is fine, but these feelings go against the validity of her point. I also learned about how important timing is in a paper. Sometimes when you write a paper too soon after an incident your feelings are still high and you can miss some major objective points that could be helpful to your paper. I think that is what happened on the paper I wrote about the homeless center.

I think, in part, it was this same ability to identify with—and then distance himself from—a classmate's essay that helped Stan revise his essay on reverse discrimination. Although he never backed away from his central point, he did acknowledge after our discussion of other student essays in which the author took an aggressive stance that maybe his tone, too, was going to "turn off some readers."

But what really struck me was Stan's final essay. He had been struggling for weeks with a project on teenage alcoholism. He had done a fair amount of research but his essay, by his own acknowledgment, was "a complete mess." It was a catalogue of facts and statistics with no clear focus or purpose. Then one day he came to class volunteering to read his latest revision:

> You met your best friend one day back in high school. You had seen him before hanging around with other kids and you never were really interested in meeting him yourself, never mind becoming best friends with him. You just didn't think that you'd get along that well.
>
> Your parents did not like him from the beginning and even tell you that you are not allowed to hang around with him. Your "old" friends tell you that your new best friend will only bring trouble and stop hanging around with him before it's too late. But you don't listen to these people. You listen instead to your football buddies who tell you that your best friend is cool and that they're friends with him also. You realize that this your chance to get into the "cool crowd."
>
> You are naturally a little shy but when you're with your best friend, you get more relaxed, even loud and obnoxious. You think that you are having a great time with this new friend. He always thinks up great tricks to play on other people and parties to go to.

The only problem is that whenever you are around him you get into trouble. You start getting headaches when you're with him and sometimes sick to your stomach. And since you've been friends, your grades start to go down. . . .

As I listened I was fairly sure I knew what had triggered Stan's new approach. One of the strongest essays in *Student Voices* was a piece by a student on her anorexia. Here is how that essay started:

You don't want to think that you're fat, you just do. Actually, you'd love it if you could accept yourself for who you are. You stop eating, no one notices until you start to lose a lot of weight. Everyday you go to lunch and eat crackers and drink skim milk. Your friends ask you, "Is that all you are going to eat?" You answer them with the obvious lie, "I'm not very hungry today." Even though your stomach has a huge knot in it, and you're so hungry that you feel nauseous. You know that you haven't eaten since lunch the day before, but no one else knows this. This whole process seems so simple to you. All you'll eat for lunch everyday is crackers, and you won't eat any other meals.

After school, you go to track practice, weak and tired. Antici- pating a tough day, your eyes fill with tears, and it takes all the courage you have to keep from crying. Your coach tells you to run six miles but you don't even feel capable of running one simple little mile. You struggle through your run, trying your best to keep up with your friends. This whole time you realize that you should have eaten more for lunch, then this run wouldn't be all that bad, but you have to lose weight and that's most important. You strain yourself day after day, feeling proud if you've avoided food completely. Your nights are simple, you take a bath and then lock yourself in your bedroom, so you won't be tempted to eat anything. When your parents ask you why you aren't eating dinner, you answer them with another lie, "I had a big lunch." The next day you go through the same routine, struggling and lying just to make it through the day. . . .

I did not want to put Stan on the spot by asking him how directly he had borrowed from this essay but his answer was on his final exam:

I can't really say that there was one specific essay that I read this semester that taught me the most about writing. But I can say that the thing that made the biggest impression on me as a writer was reading that collection of essays you published by students who took the course last year. There were a lot of pieces in that book that I modeled my writing after, like Kevin Kacin's essay on how pro- crastinating can actually help someone's writing and Marisa Kathanis' essay about why she thought her priest was a hypocrite. But Linda Denny's essay "You Don't Want to Think You're Fat, You Just Do," the one about anorexia, was the first piece that inspired me and it actually inspired my last essay. I had been thinking about teenage alcoholism all semester, but I didn't know how to write a paper on that. Then I read Linda Denny's piece and ideas just started coming to me. I wanted my piece to be as strong as hers was. Also, her piece gave me the idea of using "You" instead of "I" or "he." I like the way she started the piece; she drew the reader in by using "you." It made it seem like the paper was about each reader instead of just being about her own experience. I figured if she could make me feel what it feels like to be anorexic, then I could to that in my piece about alcoholism. But don't get the wrong idea; I did not plagiarize anything! Her essay just gave me that little push that I sometimes need, but don't always get.

Chapter Eight

Collaboration: The Case for Coauthored, Dialogic, Nonlinear Texts

I remember the day it hit me. There I was during peer editing time, frozen in my chair, uninterested in joining any of the small groups scattered around the classroom, and I was thinking, "What am I doing? Why am I sitting here watching my students waste time?" I looked around: one group was sitting in total silence, each person staring off into space; in another group, all three members were very deliberately gathering up their coats and books and staring up at the clock in preparation for a dash out the door when the class officially ended; and three other students were hunched over an essay, the two who had already finished the page waiting for the slowest reader to catch up. But then some hope: I saw a group of students in the corner talking animatedly, gesturing, all three leaning in to listen. I moved a few steps closer, hoping to catch these peer reviewers hard at exciting work, ". . . he had been trying to scoop her all night, all semester really, but they were both so blitzed, I don't think she even recognized him . . ." "NO. You're kidding! I thought he was still with Susan . . ."

Since there were still five minutes left, I decided to make one last effort. I dropped into a seat in the group who were still staring at the final page of an essay: "How's it going?" I asked, trying to sound curious but casual. "Not so great," one of them answered. "We're trying to help Jim figure out how to revise his paper. He said you told him in his conference that it needed something, but we can't think of anything to add that wouldn't ruin the point he is trying to make." I felt them all glaring at me. I looked up at the clock, waiting for it move.

How had it come to this? Why was this part of my class such a flop? Didn't these students know anything about the power of peer review? Didn't they know that when I divided them into groups of three, when I invited them to collaborate, to construct knowledge socially, to brainstorm together, when I told them that we would learn from one another in this class, I expected them to do it? Hadn't they read Ken Bruffee? Didn't they know about the Festschrift honoring Ann Berthoff? Didn't they want to become a community of writers?

Blaming students for unproductive writing relationships is always an easy place to start but never a good place to stop. Still, I was baffled and frustrated. After all, with the exception of a few thoughtful critiques (e.g, George; Gere; and Newkirk "Direction"), almost everything I have ever read and heard about group work has been glowingly positive. But too often my own experience with small-group work has been like the time I bought a gas grill from a store that was going out of business; it looked and worked great when I saw it on display, but when I got it home, I found out that the whole thing came unassembled in a large flat box with bags and bags of tiny bolts, nuts, and screws.

I know that I am overstating this: not all my peer review sessions have been failures, and there are many teachers who have found ways to make small-group work effective in their writing classes. There is even a great deal of research that explains how and why writing groups work (Bruffee; Brooke; and Gere). Nevertheless, it seems to me that over the past few years we have come dangerously close to reifying almost any classroom activity that requires students to work together in small groups—group brainstorming, peer editing, peer review—simply because most teachers in the process camp have agreed that collaboration, unlike competition, is inherently good.

While I am convinced that collaborative writing makes sense politically and pedagogically, I am not convinced that we have paid enough attention to how or why it works. Then again maybe I am just defensive because when I first confessed my problems and failures with small-group work to strong advocates of peer editing, they insisted that the problem was not with the method but with me:

> You can't just ask students to work in small groups. You have to show them how to work together.

> You can't use group work every once in a while. It takes weeks and weeks for students to learn to trust each other. You need to stick with it for a whole semester.

You have constantly to monitor every group in the room to make sure that they are on-task. You have to work harder in the peer workshop classroom than in the traditional one.

Don't allow any negative comments. Negative comments can cripple a whole group.

All of this made sense, but it all seemed so labor-intensive and so rigidly scripted that I began to have real doubts: if I had to work so hard at making my students feel like a real group, maybe they were not a real group; if I had to spend so much time telling them how to collaborate in the way that I wanted them to, wouldn't that defeat at least part of the purpose of peer group work, that is, of making them less dependent on me? And if what my students told me about competition was true, then perhaps peer editing forced students into awkward, even hypocritical, positions. In short, I worried whether peer editing placed students in unproductive relationships with me as the teacher and with one another as writers.

I want to be clear: I am certainly not suggesting that we return to traditional methods of composition instruction that isolated students and teachers, that ignored the potential power of collaboration in the classroom, and that led to small-group work in the first place. Nor am I suggesting that we return to a mindset that equates collaboration with plagiarism and cheating. (In my early days of teaching whenever I came across students whom I suspected of having worked together on their essays, I would question them separately under hot lights until I extracted a confession: "Yes, I'll admit it. We're guilty; we did help each other, but we didn't mean to.")

So in that moment when I asked myself. "What am I doing here? How did it come to this?" on some level I already knew the answer: I had turned to peer review and collaborative projects after realizing the frustrating and debilitating isolation that my students felt in my classes (see Chapter 5, for example). Like most teachers in the process camp, I have long accepted and even parroted the theoretical arguments of the social constructivists—Bruffee, Berthoff, LeFevre, and others—that the image of the writer struggling alone for inspiration and meaning is unrealistic and inhibiting; that students can learn new strategies, heuristics, and information from their peers; and that almost all "real world" writing is in some way collaborative.

But after scores of journal articles, hundreds of conference presentations, and thousands of writing workshop classes, "collaborative writing" has come to mean many different things to people in our field. Unfortunately, given the "god term" status that collaboration currently enjoys, we have done very little to separate the chaff from the wheat (or, as teachers often worry when they assign collaborative projects, the waif from the cheat). In other words, by lumping together under the heading "collaborative writing" every classroom technique that in any way requires or allows group work, we have confused one another and ourselves.

Rather than arguing for a step back to precollaborative days, what I am arguing in this chapter is that most of what we call "collaborative writing" does not go far enough. Group brainstorming and peer editing do relatively little to challenge and break down the traditional relationships between students. In most writing workshops, the finished text still belongs only to one writer and, in most cases, the evaluation that counts still belongs only to the teacher. As a result, many students still feel detached and disconnected from their peers' texts.

In some ways it was my own detachment that led me to doubt the effectiveness of frequent small-group work. And in all probability it was my own frustration that made these doubts self-fulfilling. But whether my negative attitude about peer editing was an effect or a cause of the problem ceased to matter very much. The fact is the method did not work well in my class. It got to the point that every time I asked students to work in small groups I would suddenly remember the old joke, the one in which the traditional principal stops into a process classroom and sees students working in groups and the teacher just sitting there watching and says, "I was going to observe your class; I'll come back when you're really teaching." I had always smiled at that, pretending the joke was on the principal, but suddenly it didn't seem that funny. I didn't feel that I was teaching or my students were learning all that much.

Collaborative Composing: Beyond Peer Review

If we want to create new kinds of relationships in the writing class we need to do more than tack on some student-student discussion before or after the composing occurs. In some ways, the halfhearted collaboration created by peer review seems to me the worst of both worlds—lacking the energy and honesty of intense and direct peer competition but also the intimacy and exhilaration of intense and total peer collaboration. What we often have instead of either competition or collaboration is a weird no-man's-and-woman's-land where students feign collaboration. It is a land that looks right—from a distance. Students are huddled together in small groups, talking about one another's essays. But to what extent are these students productively collaborating? As I argued in the chapter on competition, students in these sessions often hold back, consciously and unconsciously, in their advice to their peers. To what extent is it fair or reasonable to ask students to help one another when they still feel as if they are competing against one another in some sense? And I have began to wonder whether students are best served by a peer editing task that often takes their attention away from the intellectual and rhetorical problems they are working on in their own writing.

If we really want to disrupt expectations and typical peer relationships, we need to go well beyond peer review; we need to move to actual coauthorship, that is, to asking students to share responsibility for a text from topic selection through final edit. All coauthored compositions require some peer review, but not all peer review leads to coauthoring; coauthoring goes beyond peer review or peer editing, in which students read and respond to one another's writing, by requiring a group of students to write an essay together, from prewriting through final revision. By asking the students to share equal responsibility for a final product and to create an essay requiring consensus on a number of different issues, a coauthored assignment fundamentally challenges and changes the usual student-student relationship; in seeking to resolve shared problems, group members must more carefully consider alternative ideas and approaches and must learn to articulate more clearly their own presuppositions, goals, and strategies.

The main objection I hear from some of my colleagues outside the process movement to this idea of coauthoring goes something like, "Since writing is meant to be a solitary process, students should write alone." But while there is certainly value and reward in independent thinking and in developing an individual writing style, it is not true that we can gain those skills only by working alone. It is often in coauthoring that students first realize they have their own distinctive way of thinking and writing; many of my students point to that—"the realization," as one student wrote, "that there could be two or three or even twenty different ways to write a sentence or a paragraph"—as the greatest benefit of coauthoring. Certainly the experience of observing and practicing a different writing process has value for most students.

Of course, not all students make immediate, dramatic, or even conscious decisions to change their own writing process because of these observations, but some students pick up a specific technique—outlining, freewriting, organizing by comparison and contrast, for example—only after another student shows them a way to make it work. Others, as a direct result of negotiating in a coauthored project, finally come to understand the concept of audience, that written words have a purpose and an effect and that writing exists outside the student-teacher one-to-one relationship. This is not anything contrary to what I have told these same students (often more than once); the difference is that peer coauthors can sometimes teach the same thing more effectively.

Also, although I am proposing coauthoring primarily as an alternative to peer review, coauthoring can lead to an increase in the quantity and quality of peer editing that goes on in the class. Many students have trouble honestly criticizing another student's writing and many students have trouble being honestly criticized. But the whole dynamic changes in a coauthored project. If a class is asked to respond to an essay written by three students, they do not worry so much about hurting anyone's feelings and no single writer feels devastated or bitter. In fact, these discussions often lead to a sort of friendly rivalry between groups (the sort of productive hybrid of competition and collaboration that I suggested was possible in the previous chapter) and, more importantly, a shared support among coauthors. In subsequent peer editing projects many students feel freer to speak honestly and to listen openly; having been through an aggressive oral defense in the less threatening environment of the coauthored text, some students are now ready to engage in the same type of discussion one-on-one.

Finally, as a result of the close interaction with peers, students in coauthoring projects usually feel better about the writing process. A common complaint by freshmen composition students is, "I just sit in my dorm room, staring at the paper, trying to come up with a topic." As I argue in Chapter 4, a certain amount of tension or frustration is inherent and even useful in the writing process, but it becomes counterproductive at that point at which a student loses confidence and dreads every assignment. Coauthored projects allow students to work together and to support one another; they do not give them the false sense that writing is easy, but rather that they are not alone in finding it hard. But perhaps more importantly, coauthoring allows, even forces, students to develop interpersonal relationships with their peers that extend beyond the walls of the classroom and the hours of the class meetings.

Coauthoring in One Freshman Composition Class

I wanted to find out what happens to the student-student relationship during coauthoring, and so (with the assistance of a generous grant from the Fund for the Improvement of Postsecondary Education) I studied the attitudes toward and the results of a project in which groups of students wrote coauthored, nonlinear texts. Let me explain: students worked together from topic selection through final edit in groups of three. The essays were entered, shaped, revised, and negotiated on a local area computer network over a period of several weeks. All three coauthors and I had access to a word processing feature that allowed us to comment between the lines of the evolving text. These comments (which could be questions, annotations, minority reports, messages, suggestions, or complaints but were usually comments about the process of writing) could be visible or invisible on any particular reading, giving the reader the choice of reading the evolving text from start to finish or of reading deconstructively, that is, of following the nonlinear, digressive conversation that appeared in the gaps.

I know that I have suddenly introduced several new variables that may upset those looking for hard evidence about coauthoring. But if we want to see how coauthorship alters traditional classroom relationships, this kind of structure makes sense for several reasons.

First, coauthoring, creating soft-copy text on a computer screen, and nonlinear reading are naturally related because they all challenge the notion of a fixed single-authored text and a unilateral teacher-student dialogue.

Second, if we want to change writing relationships, we need to do something very different from just saying, "Why don't you students talk in groups about your writing?" I wanted my students and myself to notice and feel the difference, to be surprised, to be thrown off balance a little, to see writing as a new thing with new possibilities. In order to establish new relationships between students and texts, between students and teachers, and most of all between teachers and their peers, I needed to change a lot of things at once.

Third, the embedded, nonlinear dialogue feature probably sounds like a fad or glitzy add-on; but actually it was an attempt to respond to some of the problems created by coauthoring. As Greg Meyers and Donald Stewart, among others, have argued, consensus sometimes leaves little room for dissensus, not to mention individuality. In collaborative projects there is often little room for personal voice, style, and initiative, qualities that I stress in all other writing assignments. So I wanted to develop a project that answered the problems of coauthoring, a project in which students could write against their own text, that is, against their own group's text, as it was being written. This embedded text in which students could annotate, digress, argue, complain, ask for help, gave students access to their individual voices and gave me as the teacher access to the contribution of each student.

Finally, in order to implement such a complicated process, I needed to ask students to work on a local area computer network. I suppose it would be possible for students to create nonlinear coauthored essays without a computer, but it would require a phenomenal amount and waste of paper, paste, and patience. In my class, coauthors could talk on-line or leave me and one another text to read later in the day or later in the semester. I read and responded to the essays on-line every week or so.

The Results: Writing Between the Lines

In many ways the negotiated, linear text of these essays did not look much different from most other student essays I've read, though there was generally a narrower range in quality than in a typical batch of individual essays. I did not receive a coauthored essay that was as weak as the poorest individually composed essay. Every sloppy idea and creatively spelled word had to get by two interested critics and, as a result, there were fewer basic errors in mechanics or logic. And, because there were always two skeptics for each general assertion, there was much more evidence and support. By the same token, the coauthored essays were not as good as the very best individual essays. Missing were the distinctive voice and style that stand out in first-rate essays.

Still, I was less concerned about the quality of the finished coauthored essays than I was about the quality of the conversation and editing that produced them. My primary goal for the coauthored assignments was to get students to talk and think seriously about writing and writers' decisions and to challenge the typical student-student relationship. In some cases the hidden text—the writing between the lines—turned into extended digressions that were more interesting and thoughtful than the "primary" text. For example, these students are writing an essay examining the obligation that Saint Anselm College, a Catholic institution where I used to teach, has to its non-Catholic students:

> The next line is one of the most important in the college handbook: "It is the purpose of Saint Anselm to offer its students access to an education process which will encourage them to lead lives that are both creative and generous." Though it may not be directly stated, the non-Catholic could interpret this to mean that only those who pursue an education that is liberal in the Benedictine Catholic tradition will lead a life that is creative and generous. That is insulting to students of another faith.

Angie: But do you guys think that this is what they are trying to say?

Stu: I do not really think that this is what they are trying to say, but if someone who is not familiar with what it means to be a Benedictine reads this statement, it is sure to raise some questions. The college most likely didn't mean to give the opinion that only their education is a worthy one.

Jeremy: Stu, it is a good point you raise about it being insulting if you interpreted the quote from a certain standpoint. I think that what the quote may be saying is that [the purpose of the college] is to attempt to provide this type of education—although it is possible that a non-Catholic "could" interpret this quote that way. The problem with that interpretation is that the key word is "encourage."

Angie: Jeremy, I never thought I'd be saying this but you, as well as the others, are trying to tear the sentence apart like it was a short story. I'm sure umpteen other colleges have the same exact line. You have to consider an author's *intention,* not just the exact words.

Another group wrote a researched essay about the school's lack of adequate facilities for handicapped students. After three drafts, they decided that their dispassionate, third-person tone was not working, that their readers "just wouldn't feel the frustration and pain that a student in a wheelchair would feel if he couldn't get into some of the buildings at the school." So with three days left until the due date and with a finished (though unsatisfying) essay in hand, they agreed to start over with a first-person account of the school grounds from the perspective of a fictional character, a student in a wheelchair.

Although this may have been overly ambitious—in fact, these three writers were unable to sustain a consistent tone and style throughout the narrative—it was a decision that showed a sophisticated awareness of audience, point of view, and the revision process; given the tremendous amount of time and effort this revision required, it also showed an impressive commitment to the project and to each other.

This attitude was fairly common among the students who used nonlinear coauthoring: a reluctant pride in the process and product. I think that a large part of the project's success was due to the hidden-text option, which allowed individual group members a chance to express ideas, emotions, and concerns that for one reason or another did not fit into the coauthored essay. For example, in the following coauthored paragraph on the Joyce Carol Oates story "Where Are You Going, Where Have You Been?" one of the students used the hidden text to describe an extremely personal response:

> At this point the reader can feel trauma building as Connie no longer only dreams of boys, but thinks about this one particular man she met the previous evening. Of course, Connie wanted to sexually attract this man. She did and he arrived at her house ready for her.

Sharon: It is at this point that I feel the most for Connie. The time when you think everything is great and you've got it all under control. The shock that will hit her has hit me many times. As I read this piece of the story my stomach began to quiver and in my mind I was shouting at her "Get out of there now!!!!!!!"

> Their whole encounter is sexual, and the author wants it to be that way. It is a sexual experience for Connie, making her realize that sex is not all physical, and not everything is as it appears. Arnold Friend learns that he can manipulate this fifteen-year-old girl. When he comes to Connie's house, he thinks that he can, but when he leaves, he knows it.

Clearly, Sharon's statements are written in a very different voice than is the coauthored text to which she also contributed. That difference became the focus of productive discussions within the group not only about the purpose, tone, and point of view of both the coauthored essay and the Oates story, but also about the experiences, assumptions, and interpretive strategies each reader brings to a text.

The dynamic and character of most of the hidden-text exchanges are different from those we usually encounter in peer review sessions. There is a seriousness of thought and purpose about the project but at the same time the exchanges have a relaxed, casual tone (as this embedded conversation indicates):

> Guys—I read another article about how Marx wrote *The Communist Manifesto* and I added some stuff to the end. See if you like it. Feel free to trash anything or to put in some more stuff if you think it needs it.—Liz

> Mike and Liz, we need more input on why studying politics is important. What do you think of the stuff so far? It's very rough. Try to elaborate on anything you feel needs to be stretched.—Jean

> This seems really good so far. I'll go through it again and try to add some more.—Mike

> Mike, we like what you changed, but don't you think that grammatically it needs work? Do you like the parts that we put in about the nature of politics in relation to Marx and a liberal arts education?—Liz and Jean

> Liz and Jean, I like it a lot. Thanks. I'll make sure to use the spell check and try to fix any little mistakes before we hand it in.—Mike

I do not mean to suggest that every interaction was as supportive and as gracious as these examples might indicate. There were a number of conflicts and breakdowns within certain groups. But often those conflicts were played out in the hidden text in a way that demonstrated a mutual understanding and comfortableness in the relationship. This group is negotiating a text about the role of science in a liberal arts curriculum:

Beth: Hi guys. I was always told that science increased your curiosity in the world around you. It is supposed to increase your power of investigation. I think the reason that science is taught at a liberal arts college is because I think it is necessary to have at least a general idea about the human body and how it works. I think it is necessary because we are all human and each and every one of us is composed of the same basic unit. I think it is interesting to know that all creatures, at least mammals, all run basically the same way and have similar body systems (nervous, digestive, circulatory, etc.).

Now, Kaitlin, don't say that I'm getting all excited over this just because it is my major. Didn't you enjoy your general biology course? Don't say you didn't because I know you did. Well guys. This is just a little tidbit of information. I am curious to find out what you think about science, from a non-major's point of view? Why do you think you had to have a year of science? I'll talk to you later.

Jim: Well peoples—as usual I'll tie God into this somehow—science can also be viewed as an extension of God. If God is in fact part of all things then he would also be part of science and one could find something about the nature of God by studying his creations.

Beth and Kaitlin: Torborg, we hate you!!!!!!!! O.K. Torborg you tell us what you want and we will try to see it your way. You have totally confused us now thank you. Are you talking about just Catholic liberal arts colleges or liberal arts colleges in general.

Jim: I'm talking in general because I really don't think that the non-Catholic ones care about the nature of God when they are studying science.

Beth and Kaitlin: The question is why have science in the required curriculum of a liberal arts college, not what the connection is between God and science. This collaborative stuff really frustrates us and we can't take any more of it at the present time. We will be back later after we calm down. Our intentions were good. Oh, by the way Jim, we used to like you before we took on this collaborative relationship. Maybe we three should go for some counseling to deal with this traumatic experience that has effected our lives permanently. The sight of you scares us!!!!!!! With deepest concern, your coauthors.

Jim: Well, Beth and Kaitlin, this definitely sounds like a personal problem to me but we should try to make do since we do have a grade riding on this: if you two would like to stick to strictly a general everyday liberal arts college I suppose we can do that except that I believe there must be more of a reason to include science than just the fact that we should know something about our bodies. P.S.—By the way, thanks for your lovely note.

Another group spent several pages arguing about whether Lotte and Werther's relationship in Goethe's *Sorrows of Young Werther* was healthy or unhealthy. Finally, the group members decided they could not determine this until they first established some criteria for a healthy relationship.

> A happy, healthy relationship compared to the relationship in question involves all the qualities that Werther and Lotte lacked. Communication, an important asset to any relationship, was the deficiency that cost a life. Werther acted on feelings and erratic emotions. He felt that Lotte would come to him and unfortunately his desires controlled his actions. A good relationship involves two people who have mutual feelings, are well-balanced, respect and trust each other. In the case of Werther and Lotte there wasn't mutuality and, due to the lack of communication and honesty, this was not clearly stated, causing Werther to misconstrue the true feelings Lotte had for him. Therefore, it is obvious that Werther had an unhealthy relationship based on obsession and unrealistic goals. If the relationship possessed positive qualities such as clear, concise communication and mutuality, perhaps Werther would not have sought suicide as a solution.

Craig: At first we couldn't agree about what was a healthy relationship, but that was because we had two males and one female in the group and we realized that men and women look at relationships differently. Once we talked that out we figured out what we wanted to say. We never could have written this paper individually because we would have had a biased male or biased female viewpoint.

The exchanges between these students seem to me halfway between casual spoken comments and more formal written responses. Perhaps most importantly, they seem the comments of one writer to another writer. And of one reader to another reader. In fact, these students are coming to see the reading process in new ways. By developing more productive relationships with one another, they are also developing more productive relationships with written texts. Too many beginning students think of written texts only as stable, finished products. By working with other writers to create a layered, dynamic text, students realize that writing is an organic and dialogic process. Because the hidden text can be embedded into a page, paragraph, or sentence and appears on the screen exactly where it is inserted, students are given the chance to reconsider their evolving text as it is constructed and—literally—deconstructed. Students then realize that there is not just one "correct" way to write a particular paragraph or essay. For some, this realization leads to a sense of liberation, even playfulness, not only in their writing but in their reading of literary texts as well.

When the project was completed, I asked these students if it was worth it. One of the students in this group offered what I take to be the definitive backhanded compliment:

> I don't know. It was too much work. First, we had to choose a topic, then a point of view, and then we had to figure out how to divide up the work. And we had to set up some meetings after class to go over everything and to talk everything out. And then when we were almost done, we realized that our point of view wasn't working for the audience. So we had to figure out how to make an audience see our argument the way we wanted them to see it. By the end we must have put in about ten hours each, which is thirty hours altogether. I mean I never could have written something like this by myself; it turned out to be a good paper and I am prouder of this essay than all the rest I've written in this class. But I don't know . . . when I write an essay by myself the whole thing never takes me more than thirty minutes.

Part Three

The Teacher-Teacher Relationship

At the beginning of this book, I argue that we need some way to limit our working definition of "context" as it relates to composition classes. Toward that end, I suggest that we focus particularly on the interpersonal relationships within the classroom that shape reading and writing. There are, however, all sorts of relationships that students and teachers have with people *outside* the classroom—parents, siblings, employers, roommates, etc.—that also shape academic writing and reading. I've nevertheless decided to limit my study to the three relationships—teacher-student, student-student, and teacher-teacher—that I believe have the most direct impact on what goes on inside the writing class.

I've done this not only because of the practical limitations I face as a writer (each student's roommate and parents have relationships of their own with people who have relationships with people who have relationships, and on and on), but also because of the practical demands I anticipate of my readers. In other words, since I see my audience first as teachers and second as researchers, I have consciously decided to focus on relationships within the shared and familiar territory of the classroom.

You may well ask how I can include the teacher-teacher relationship *within* the classroom. Our colleagues are hardly ever present when we teach; in fact, one writing program administrator once complained to me, "It's so awkward doing classroom observations of my staff; if I walk unannounced into another teacher's classroom, I get a look like I just barged into their bedroom." Still, while our colleagues are not literally present in our classrooms, we are almost always aware of their presence, aware of how our attitude and our approach, our goals and our grades, compare with theirs.

Our peers' influence on us is in many ways as powerful and as complex as student writers' influence on one another. Oddly enough, there is very little composition scholarship available about any of the issues raised by the teacher-teacher relationship. And it is that relationship—the one that any writing teacher has to her colleagues in her department and in her discipline—that provides the context and often the direction for the teacher-student and student-student relationships in the class. While it is by now a commonplace of composition theory to say that many student writers fail because they feel isolated in their classroom and confused by the conventions of the discourse community they are trying to enter, there is almost no work about the extent to which writing teachers feel isolated and confused and even less about how these negative feelings manifest themselves in the classroom.

We seem to be avoiding some crucial questions. How do our relationships (or lack of relationships) with colleagues shape our interactions with students? To what extent are we (or *should* we be) a unified or at least coherent group or community? What issues do we need to talk about *with other*—in our department meetings, coffee shops, national conferences, and academic journals—before we can talk about them effectively with our students? In short, how can we develop peer relationships that provide the motivation, information, and support necessary to keep the reading and writing processes alive?

The answers, I think, are surprisingly similar to those I offer in the chapters on the teacher-student and student-student relationships: if we want to become better writing teachers, we need to develop better writing relationships; and if we want to develop better writing relationships, we need to start by carefully examining, analyzing, and telling stories about the peer relationships that currently exist in our departments and in our discipline.

Chapter Nine

Voices in My Head, Fairy Tales I Still Believe, and Other Topics Not Fit for Academic Discourse

When my first daughter was about five, she had a friend named Leah who used to come over to play. One day Leah brought a book with her—*Snow White*—which the girls asked me to read. The story went pretty much as I remembered and expected until I got to the part where the evil stepmother tells her hunter to take Snow White into the woods and kill her. The words describing this scene were crossed out and someone—Leah's mother, it turned out—had written a kinder, gentler version. Something like: "Take Snow White out into the woods for a walk." Throughout the rest of the book, Leah's mother struggled valiantly against the illustrations to tell her daughter an untraumatic—and undramatic—story.

That night my wife and I weighed the pros and prose of this revisionary version; while we could certainly understand and relate to this mother's desire to protect her daughter from the world's sad and scary truths, it seemed so silly and so obviously doomed (and not just because we had to keep shushing our own streetwise five-year-old, who wanted to tell Leah the "real story"). I suspect that on some level Leah already knew the real story; like everyone else, she already had fears and fantasies that were at least as sad and as scary as the ones in *Snow White*. I wondered whether the G-rated retelling had more to do with the mother's discomfort than the daughter's fragile psyche.

I've been wondering about some of the same issues in this book, for I am convinced that we in the process movement have written our own basalized story of our classrooms. It is a story in which the

143

problems we face are manageable, if not harmless, and the solutions we offer are effective, if not brilliant. Like Leah's mother, process teachers have written a text about peer review, one-to-one conferences, invention strategies, and collaboration that is safe and clean and friendly. The enemy is traditional teaching and teachers; the heroes are—well, *we* are the heroes. The only problem is that, like Leah's mother, we face a nagging problem: this happy talk does not match the pictures and does not reflect much of what happens in our classrooms or the way we actually feel about our day-to-day teaching.

There are, of course, some good reasons for focusing on the positive, not the least of which is that we need to convince traditional teachers, administrators, and ourselves that what we are doing makes sense. And the writing process movement *has* been a kind of fairy tale. I say that not to imply that it is false or childish or naive but rather to suggest that it is a narrative about people—teachers and students—who have achieved a measure of self-actualization, even transformation and transcendence, through confronting and, often, overcoming serious obstacles. I mean that the process movement is a fairy tale in the best sense—a story that tells us, yes, it is dangerous out there but we are not alone in facing that danger and, if we persevere, we can triumph in the end.

To appreciate the triumph, we need to acknowledge and confront the extent of the difficulties we face. And, in our professional or scholarly relationships anyway, we have been reluctant to do that. We have too often presented conference papers and published journal articles and textbooks that oversimplify the problems and solutions in the teaching of writing; that is, we have too often looked at the composing process and the teaching of writing outside the context in which they occur—the context of interpersonal relationships. As I suggest in the introduction to this chapter, there is very little published material on how relationships between teachers and students and between teachers and other teachers shape reading and writing—and there is almost nothing on the most highly charged of the emotions inherent in these relationships, such as envy, competition, and sexual tension.

Why not? Why haven't we been more honest about how hard it is to teach writing? Why don't we tell each other more stories about how stressful and messy and unsettling this job can be? First, the philosophy and rhetoric of most process teaching simply assumes that this approach naturally fosters positive, supportive relationships. As opposed to traditional teachers in traditional classrooms, whom we see as isolating and mistreating their students, we see ourselves as protectors and saviors, offering support, compassion, camaraderie. It is for this reason that many of us have written articles and presented papers not as skeptics or observers but as advocates, if not disciples, of this particular pedagogical approach. In other words, because we often feel compelled to promote and defend our own teaching methods and our own research findings, we too often fail to admit our failures and, thus, face too many complicated issues alone and unprepared. I am not talking about the need for agreement on all teaching methods—that is not possible or even desirable—but about the need for more honest and rich discussion and debate.

The teaching of writing has been and continues to be highly politicized within English departments and within the profession, and while those politics have tended to energize our discipline, they have also created a certain amount of defensiveness and resistance. Given this climate, it is not easy to admit our weaknesses and vulnerabilities, unless we know in advance that our listeners have the same (or at least equally daunting) weaknesses and vulnerabilities. And so we spend much too much time and energy in our professional relationships protecting our turf, our particular pedagogical approach, and perhaps most of all our ego. Not only does this keep us from learning new strategies for teaching and research, it also keeps us from relating honestly to each other.

The solution? We need to stop pretending that we always have everything under control, that everything is proceeding according to plan. (Maybe I should have started this chapter with *The Emperor's New Clothes* rather than *Snow White*.) In other words, we need to stop pretending that we are always objective readers of student texts; that writing—for our students and for ourselves—is always a journey of discovery; that peer review is always positive and helpful; that writing workshops create noncompetitive communities; that teachers can decentralize authority in their classrooms by simple decree; and so on. As soon as we stop talking about idealized classrooms and start talking about our students and ourselves, we are forced to confront the tension, competition, misunderstanding, frustration, resistance, and disappointment that are inevitable aspects not only of the writing process but also of the relationships that are established within the writing class.

Acknowledging the powerful and sometimes negative feelings that are produced even (or especially) in process-oriented writing classrooms is not an easy step but one we must take if this movement is to survive. I have tried in this book to "problematize" the process paradigm, not because I reject it but because I accept it and because I think it needs more depth, more honesty, more sophistication, than we, its advocates, have so far provided. But in order to accomplish this, we will, necessarily, be forced to take ourselves—our strengths and our weaknesses—into account in a way that is more honest and thorough than we have done before. We will need to establish new models not only for teacher-student and student-student relationships but also for teacher-teacher relationships.

I am aware that some readers may feel we would do better to focus on strategies for teaching writing or on research on composing rather than on professional self-examination, but again these choices are not mutually exclusive. My sense is that many of us have trouble dealing with students, trouble staying motivated, trouble locating our audience, because we lack productive peer relationships in the department and in the field.

Here, too, my research is largely autobiographical. For a number of years I taught in a composition program that provided me with very little guidance, moral support, prestige, or pay, and I am absolutely convinced that much of the alienation from—and frustration with—my students I felt during that period was directly related to my lack of productive peer relationships. In fact, there was a period in my early years of teaching during which most of my peer interactions were contentious. I was aware that many of my colleagues disapproved of my classroom approach; they expected me to teach more conventionally, to emphasize correctness more and personal expression less. And so, in a complicated way, I was often talking to—arguing against—these colleagues through my students. For example, if a student questioned one of my assignments, I would often respond defensively or belligerently, at least in part because I was continuing an ongoing argument with a colleague. (I think that my charged response to Steve's approach to research writing is a clear example of this dynamic at work.)

Ironically, my frustration during this period was similar in many ways to my students'. Because I was one of a number of part-time writing teachers worried about keeping my job, I was anxious about assessment (what criteria would the chairperson use to determine which of us would get contracts for the following year?) and competitive with some of my colleagues; I was not always sure what was expected of me or even who expected it (who was my audience, anyway? my students? my chairperson? the dean?); I was reluctant to admit how much I didn't know, how hard I felt it was to teach writing, how much I needed advice, commiseration, and moral support. Much like the students I describe in Chapter 2, I was insecure about my ability and angry at the authority figures who reminded me of that insecurity.

Part of the problem was that many of the full-time English faculty were interested only in literature and had little or no respect for the teaching of writing or for those who were trying to teach it. It is not surprising, then, that I found some of my first supportive colleagues through professional contacts, that is, though conferences and journals. My attitude and behavior in my own classroom began to change when I began to attend national conferences and to read widely in the field. It was only when I began to see myself as part of a supportive community that I had the confidence to acknowledge my weaknesses and to try new approaches in the classroom. I began to view and listen to my conversations with students in terms of the conversations I was having with colleagues and vice versa. I began to think about assignments that I used for years in new ways. Was I overemphasizing personal narrative at the expense of academic discourse? How could I pay attention to individual voices and the social construction of knowledge at the same time?

But the real transformation in my relationships with students came as a result of my own research and my writing about that research. A number of edited collections (Goswami and Stillman, Bissex and Bullock, Daiker and Morenberg) have focused on how teacher research provides information we do not get from other approaches and how it changes a teacher's self-image, but none have looked carefully enough at how this in turn changes classroom relationships and teaching.

Becoming a teacher researcher is bound to change a teacher's relationships with students in fundamental ways. In some sense, the student becomes a subject first and a student (or person) second. As cold as that sounds, the irony is that I became more engaged, more attentive, more sensitive, when I was dealing with the students who were my research subjects for this book. But this engagement or relationship, like all the relationships in this book, is complicated. On the one hand, there is the danger that we will exploit and manipulate our case study subjects, that we will teach and respond to them in ways that further our own research and theory. At the same time, our dependence on their involvement and openness in our project makes us indebted to them and vulnerable to some extent to *their* manipulation.

Be that as it may, I began to relate more effectively to my students because I had a more productive relationship with my peers, and more effectively to my peers because I had a more productive relationship with my students. Since I realize that I am beginning to sound an awful lot like the happy talkers I have been criticizing, let me quickly add that these new relationships were more productive partly because I could finally admit what was *not* working in my classroom. As strange as it sounds, I think I became a better teacher once I could admit to my peers that I was not a very good one. As daunting as the difficulties we face as writing teachers are, I have found they become much more manageable when I've been able to discuss them with my colleagues down the hall.

The irony, of course, is that these colleagues have been there all along; I've always heard their voices—at least the voices I've invented for them—in my head. I now realize that I was too proud, too scared, too guarded, to talk to them honestly about what it felt like to teach writing: I was too busy trying to fool them into thinking that I already knew damn well what I was doing. The truth is I often don't know. In fact, whenever I face a difficult decision or moment—when Polly bursts into tears in the middle of her conference, when I think Steve's essay is anti-Semitic, when I give out a set of grades that is much higher or much lower than the norm—I find myself wondering what my colleagues might think or say about the situation and yearning for their guidance and support.

In order to become more effective in my relationships with students, I needed to establish better peer relationships and I did that by replacing the imagined voices of disapproval or derision with real voices and opinions and suggestions. This doesn't mean only that we need colleagues who are friends, though that is certainly part of it; in my case, it means that I have found colleagues with whom I teach ("what would Tom or Libby do in this situation?"); colleagues against whom I teach (the teacher with whom I shared an office who talked constantly about what her students couldn't do and who measured the margins of each term paper with a ruler); and even some colleagues, such as Don Murray, with *and* against whom I teach (see Chapters 3 and 6 for illustration).

Like my students, I have found benefit in having a range of peer relationships: I have colleagues I admire; colleagues I hope admire me; colleagues I envy; colleagues whose students I pity; colleagues with whom I can commiserate about my problems, concerns, and failings; colleagues with whom I collaborative; colleagues against whom I compete in the classroom, in department meetings, and in print; colleagues with whom I identify; colleagues I use as models. Like the other relationships I describe in this book, the teacher-teacher relationship shapes much of the writing and reading in every classroom; like the other relationships I describe in this book, the teacher-teacher relationship needs to be constantly monitored, so that here, too, we are working not in a void but in a state of productive tension.

I know the thought of trying to keep track of all these relationships and to teach writing at the same time may seem mind-boggling, but keeping track of all these relationships *is* teaching writing. We have told each other and ourselves stories about the teaching of writing that do not allow enough room for mind-boggling complexity or ambivalent feelings, let alone our own fantasies about the witches and hunters who wait for *us* in the dark woods.

I am not saying that it is time to stop telling each other fairy tales or even that we should change the happy ending; I'm well aware of the remarkable progress we have made as teachers and our students have made as writers as a result of this more dynamic, process approach. I *am* saying it is time to move beyond the *edited* fairy tale, the basal reader of our own teaching experience. Like any good narrative, this new story will be a bit unsettling, sometimes even downright scary. But that's all right: as long as we keep telling it to each other rather than keeping it to ourselves, we'll be strong enough to take it.

Works Cited

Anderson, Worth, Cynthia Best, Alycia Black, John Hurst, Brandt Miller, and Susan Miller. "Cross-Curricular Underlife: A Collaborative Report on Ways with Academic Words." *College Composition and Communication* 41 (1990):11–36.

Aristotle. *The Rhetoric of Aristotle.* Ed. and trans. Lane Cooper. New York: Appleton-Century-Crofts, 1960.

Barker, Thomas, and Fred Kemp. "Network Theory: A Postmodern Pedagogy for the Writing Classroom." *Computers and Community: Teaching Composition in the Twenty-first Century.* Ed. Carolyn Handa. 1–27. Portsmouth, NH: Boynton/Cook, 1990.

Bartholomae, David, and Anthony Petrosky. *Facts, Artifacts, and Counterfacts: Theory and Method for a Reading and Writing Course.* Portsmouth, NH: Boynton/Cook, 1986.

Belenky, Mary F., Blythe M. Clinchy, Nancy Rule Goldberger, and Jull M. Tarule. *Women's Ways of Knowing: The Development of Self, Voice, and Mind.* New York: Basic Books, 1986.

Berlin, James. "Contemporary Composition: The Major Pedagogical Theories." *The Writing Teacher's Sourcebook.* Ed. Gary Tate and Edward P. J. Corbett. 47–59. New York: Oxford UP, 1988.

Berthoff, Ann E. *Forming/Thinking/Writing: The Composing Imagination.* Portsmouth, NH: Boynton/Cook, 1982.

Bissex, Glenda. "Why Case Studies?" *Seeing for Ourselves: Case Study Research by Teachers of Writing.* Ed. Glenda Bissex and Richard Bullock. 7–20. Portsmouth, NH: Heinemann, 1987.

Bizzell, Patricia. "Cognition, Convention, and Certainty: What We Need to Know About Writing." *Pre/Text* 3 (1982).

Booth, Wayne C. "Metaphor as Rhetoric: The Problem of Evaluation." *On Metaphor.* Ed. Sheldon Sacks. 47–70. Chicago: U of Chicago P, 1978.

Brannon, Lil, and C. H. Knoblauch. "On Students' Rights to Their Own Texts: A Model of Teacher Response." *College Composition and Communication* 33 (1982):157–66.

Brooke, Robert. "Lacan, Transference, and Writing Instruction." *College English* 49 (1987):679–91.

———. "Modeling a Writer's Identity: Reading and Imitation in the Writing Clasroom." *College Composition and Communication* 39 (1988):23–41.

———. *Writing and Sense of Self: Identity Negotiation in Writing Workshops.* Urbana: NCTE, 1991.

———. "Underlife and Writing Instruction." *College Composition and Communication* 38 (1987):141–53.

Bruffee, Kenneth. "Collaborative Learning and the 'Conversation of Mankind.' " *College English* 46 (1984):635–52.

Burke, Kenneth. *A Rhetoric of Motives.* Berkley: U of California P, 1989.

Carnicelli, Thomas. *The Writing Conference: A One-to-One Conversation." Eight Approaches to Composition.* Ed. Timothy R. Donovan and Ben W. McClelland. 101–32. Urbana, IL: NCTE, 1980.

Clark, William. "How to Completely Individualize a Writing Program." *To Compose: Teaching Writing in High School and College.* Ed. Thomas Newkirk. 2nd ed. 53–60. Portsmouth, NH: Heinemann, 1990.

Csikszentmihalyi, Mihali. *Beyond Boredom and Anxiety.* San Francisco: Jossey-Bass, 1975.

Daiker, Donald, and Max Morenberg, eds. *The Writing Teacher as Researcher: Essays in the Theory and Practice of Class-Based Research.* Portsmouth, NH: Boynton/Cook, 1990.

Dillard, Annie. "To Fashion a Text." *Inventing the Truth: The Art and Craft of Memoir.* Ed. William Zinsser. 53–76. Boston: Houghton Mifflin, 1987.

———. "Sight into Insight." *The Conscious Reader.* Ed. Caroline Shrodes et al. 3rd ed. 689–98. New York: Macmillian Publishing, 1985.

Eagleton, Terry. *Literary Theory: An Introduction.* Minneapolis: Minnesota UP, 1983.

Elbow, Peter. "Embracing Contraries in the Writing Process." *College English* 45 (1983):327–39.

———. *Writing Without Teachers.* New York: Oxford UP, 1979.

Elfenbein, Anna Shannon. "Competition: The Worm in the Bud in a Collaborative Seminar." Paper presented at the Conference on College Composition and Communication, Chicago, 1990.

Emig, Janet. "The Uses of the Unconscious in Composing." *The Web of Meaning: Essays on Writing, Teaching, Learning, and Thinking.* 44–53. Portsmouth, NH: Boynton/Cook, 1983.

Faigley, Lester. "Judging Writing, Judging Selves." *College Composition and Communication* 40 (1989):395–413.

Farber, Jerry. "Learning How to Teach: A Progress Report." *College English* 52 (1990):135–41.

Fish, Stanley. *Is There a Text in This Class?: The Authority of Interpretive Communities.* Cambridge: Harvard UP, 1980.

Flower, Linda. "Cognition, Context, and Theory Building." *College Composition and Communication* 40 (1989):282–311.

Flower, Linda, and John R. Hayes. "The Cognition of Discovery: Defining a Rhetorical Problem." *The Writing Teacher's Sourcebook.* Ed. Gary Tate and Edward P.J. Corbett. 2nd ed. 92–102. New York: Oxford UP, 1988.

Flynn, Elizabeth. "Composing as a Woman." *College Composition and Communication* 39 (1988):423–35.

Freud, Sigmund. "The Future Prospects of Psycho-Analytic Therapy." *Standard Edition of the Complete Works of Sigmund Freud.* Ed. James Strachey. Vol. XI. 144–45. London: Hogarth Press, 1957.

Fulwiler, Toby. "Freshman Writing: It's the Best Course in the University to Teach." *Composition and Literature: Exploring the Human Experience.* Ed. Jesse Jones, Veva Vonler, and Janet Harris. 17–20. San Diego: Harcourt Brace Jovanovich, 1987.

Garrison, Roger. "One-to-One: Tutorial Instruction in Freshman Composition." *New Directions for Community Colleges* 2, (1974):55–84.

George, Diana. "Working With Peer Groups in the Composition Classroom." *College Composition and Communication* 35 (1984):320–26.

Gere, Anne Ruggles. *Writing Groups: History, Theory, and Implications.* Carbondale: Southern Illinois UP, 1987.

Gilligan, Carol. *In a Different Voice: Psychological Theory and Women's Development.* Cambridge: Harvard UP, 1982.

Golding, William. *Lord of the Flies.* New York: Coward-McCann, 1962.

Goswami, Dixie, and Peter Stillman, eds. *Reclaiming the Classroom: Teacher Research as an Agency for Change.* Portsmouth, NH: Boynton/Cook, 1987.

Graves, Donald. *Writing: Teachers and Children at Work.* Portsmouth, NH: Heinemann, 1983.

Harris, Joseph. "The Plural Text/The Plural Self: Roland Barthes and William Coles." *College English* 49 (1987):158ff.

Harris, Muriel. *Teaching One-to-One: The Writing Conference.* Urbana, IL: NCTE, 1986.

Hashimoto, I. "Voice as Juice: Some Reservations About Evangelic Composition." *College Composition and Communication* 38 (1987):70–80.

———. *Thirteen Weeks.* Portsmouth, NH: Boynton/Cook, 1992.

Hawthorne, Nathaniel. *The Scarlet Letter.* New York: Norton, 1961.

Hubbuch Susan. "Confronting the Power in Empowering Students." *The Writing Instructor* 9 (1990):35–44.

Keller, Evelyn Fox, and Helene Moglen. "Competition: A Problem for Academic Women." *Competition: A Feminist Taboo?* Ed. Valerie Miner and Helen Longino. 21–37. New York: The Feminist Press, 1987.

Kozinski, Jerzy. *Being There.* New York: Harcourt Brace Jovanovich, 1971.

Lawson, Bruce, and Susan Sterr Ryan. "Introduction: Interpretative Issues in Student Writing." *Encountering Student Texts: Interpretative Issues in Reading Student Writing.* vii–xvii. Urbana, IL: NCTE, 1989.

LeFevre, Karen Burke. *Invention as a Social Act.* Carbondale: Southern Illinois UP, 1987.

Macrorie, Ken. *The I-Search Paper.* Rev. ed. of *Searching Writing.* Portsmouth, NH: Boynton/Cook, 1988.

———. *Writing to Be Read.* 3rd ed. Portsmouth, NH: Boynton Cook, 1984.

McKay, Ferguson. "Roles and Strategies in College Writing Conferences." *Seeing for Ourselves: Case Study Research by Teachers of Writing.* Ed. Glenda Bissex and Richard Bullock. Portsmouth, NH: Heinemann, 1987.

McLeod, Susan. "Some Thoughts about Feelings: The Affective Domain and the Writing Process." *College Composition and Communication* 38 (1987):426–35.

Melville. *Moby-Dick.* New York: Norton, 1967.

Meyers, Greg. "Reality, Consensus, and Reform in the Rhetoric of Composition Teaching." *College English* 48 (1986):154–74.

Miller, Susan. "The Feminization of Composition." *The Politics of Writing Instruction: Postsecondary.* Ed. Richard Bullock and John Trimbur. Portsmouth, NH: Boynton/Cook, 1991. 39–54.

Miner, Valerie. "Rumors From the Cauldron: Competition Among Feminist Writers," *Competition: A Feminist Taboo?* Ed. Valerie Miner and Helen Longino. 183–94. New York: The Feminist Press, 1987.

Moffett, James. "Writing, Inner Speech, and Mediation." *Coming on Center: Essays in English Education.* 2nd ed. Portsmouth, NH: Boynton/Cook, 1988.

Murphy, Ann. "Transference and Resistance in the Basic Writing Classroom: Problematics and Praxis." *College Composition and Communication* 40 (1989):175–87.

Murray, Donald. *A Writer Teaches Writing.* 2nd ed. Boston: Houghton, 1985.

———. *Learning By Teaching: Selected Articles on Writing and Teaching.* Portsmouth, NH: Boynton/Cook, 1982.

———. "The Listening Eye: Reflections on the Writing Conference." *The Writing Teacher's Sourcebook.* Ed. Gary Tate and Edward Corbett. 232–37. New York: Oxford UP, 1968.

———. "Waiting for Writing." *Shoptalk: Learning to Write with Writers.* Ed. Donald Murray. 69–79. Portsmouth, NH: Boynton/Cook. 1990.

Newkirk, Thomas. "Direction and Misdirection in Peer Response." *College Composition and Communication* 35 (1984):319–29.

North, Stephen. *The Making of Knowledge in Composition: Portrait of an Emerging Field.* Portsmouth, NH: Boynton/Cook, 1987.

Onore, Cynthia. "The Student, the Teacher, and the Text; Negotiating Meanings Through Response and Revision." *Writing and Response: Theory,*

Practice, and Research. Ed. Chris M. Anson. 231– 60. Urbana, IL: NCTE, 1989.

Ong, Walter. "The Writer's Audience Is Always a Fiction." *PMLA* 90. (1975): 9–21.

Ortner, Sherry. "Is Female to Male as Nature Is to Culture?" Woman, Culture & Society. Ed. Michelle Zimbalist Roasaldo and Louise Lamphere. 67–87. Stanford: Stanford UP, 1974.

Orwell, George. "Shooting an Elephant." In Depth: Essayists for Our Time. 523–30. Fort Worth, TX: Harcourt Brace Jovanovich, 1993.

Perelman, Chaim. The Realm of Rhetoric. Trans. Wiliam Kluback, 1977. Notre Dame, Ind: U of Notre Dame P, 1982.

Perelman, Les. "The Context of Classroom Writing." College English 48 (1986):471–79.

Perl, Sondra. "Understanding Composing." College Composition and Communication 31 (1980):363–69

Peterson, Linda. "Repetition and Metaphor in the Early Stages of Composing." College Composition and Communication 36 (1985):429–43.

Phelps, Louise Wetherbee. "Images of Student Writing: The Deep Structure of Teacher Response." Writing and Response: Theory, Practice, and Research. 37–67. Ed. Chris M. Anson. Urbana, Il: NCTE, 1989.

Quintilian. Institutio Oratoria. Trans. H. E. Butler. 4 vols. Cambridge: Harvard UP, 1922.

Richards, Pamela. "Risk." Writing for Social Scientists: How to Start and Finish Your Thesis, Book, or Article. Howard S. Becker, with a chapter by Pamela Richards. 108–20. Chicago: U of Chicago P, 1986.

Romano, Tom. Clearing the Way: Working With Teenage Writers. Portsmouth, NH: Heinemann, 1990.

Ronald, Kate. "Personal and Public Authority in Discourse: Beyond Subjective/Objective Dichotomies." Farther Along: Transforming Dichotomies in Rhetoric and Composition. Ed. Kate Ronald and Hephzibah Roskelly. 1–27. Portsmouth, NH: Boynton/Cook, 1990.

Rose, Mike. Writer's Block: The Cognitive Dimension. Carbondale: Southern Illinois UP, 1984.

Rosenblatt, Louise. Literature as Exploration. NY: Modern Language Association, 1938.

Scholes, Robert. Textual Power: Literary Theory and the Teaching of English. New Haven: Yale UP, 1985.

Schuster, Charles. "The Politics of Promotion." The Politics of Writing Instruction: Postsecondary. Ed. Richard Bullock and John Trimbur. 85–96. Portsmouth, NH: Boynton/Cook, 1991.

Schwegler, Robert. "The Politics of Reading Student Papers." The Politics of Writing Instruction: Postsecondary. Ed. Richard Bullock and John Trimbur. 227–46. Portsmouth, NH: Boynton/Cook, 1991.

Shaughnessy, Mina. *Errors and Expectations: A Guide for the Teacher of Basic Writing.* New York: Oxford UP, 1977.

Smith, Louise. "Enigma Variations: Reading and Writing Through Metaphor." *Only Connect: Uniting Reading and Writing.* Ed. Thomas Newkirk. 158–73. Portsmouth, NH: Boynton/Cook. 1986.

Sommers, Nancy, and Donald McQuade, eds. *Student Writers at Work and in the Company of Other Writers: The Bedford Prizes.* New York: St. Martin, 1986.

Stafford, William. Quoted in *Shoptalk: Learning to Write with Writers.* Donald Murray. 76. Portsmouth, NH: Boynton/Cook, 1990.

Stewart, Donald. "Collaborative Learning and Composition: Boon or Bane." *Rhetoric Review* 7.1 (1988):58–83.

Strunk, William, and E. B. White. *The Elements of Style.* 3d ed. New York: Macmillan, 1979.

Thoreau, Henry David. *Walden.* New York: Random House, 1991.

Tobin, Lad. "Briding Gaps: Analyzing Student Metaphors for Composing.: *College Composition and Communication* 40 (1989):444–58.

White, E. B. "Once More to the Lake." *Essays of E. B. White.* New York: Harper Colphon Books, 1977.

Vygotsky, Lev. *Mind in Society: The Development of Higher Psychological Processes.* Ed. Michael Cole, Vera John-Steiner, Sylvia Scribner, Ellen Souberman. Cambridge UP, 1978.

Zelnick, Stephen. "Student Worlds in Student Conferences." *Writing Talks: Views on Teaching Writing from Across the Professions.* Ed. Muffy E. A. Siegal and Toby Olson. 47–58. Portsmouth, NH: Boynton/Cook, 1983.